PRAISE FOR

Pitch Secrets A to Z

"I've shared the stage, the studio, and the spotlight with Forbes Riley more times than I can count—and she's the real deal. Nobody brings passion, precision, and persuasion to a pitch like Forbes. Her energy is electric, her delivery razor-sharp, and her heart exactly where it belongs. *Pitch Secrets A to Z* bottles her brilliance. Want to learn from the best? Start here. I've seen her in action—now you get her magic, step by step."

—Beau Rials

LEGENDARY PITCHMAN & TV HOST

"Forbes Riley has an uncanny ability to light up any stage and infuse her electric energy in the audience. I've watched her magic inspire young entrepreneurs from nervous to next-level in just minutes at my annual LEAP program for students 15-25+. Although she is known world-wide as the Queen of PITCH she doesn't just teach how to pitch—she empowers. *Pitch Secrets A to Z* captures that same electric energy. If you want to present with power, purpose, and presence, this will be your Holy Grail."

—Dr. Bill Dorfman

FEATURED DENTIST ON ABC'S *EXTREME MAKEOVER*, CBS' *THE DOCTORS*, & *NEW YORK TIMES* BESTSELLING AUTHOR

"Forbes Riley and I recently wrapped filming together on my Western action film *Black Creek*, and let me tell you—she brings the same unstoppable energy to a movie set that she brings to the stage. I've seen her grab the attention of a room as fast as I can draw a sword on screen, and that's saying something.

In *Pitch Secrets A to Z*, Forbes distills that rare combination of precision, charisma, and heart into a guide that will teach you how to command any audience. Whether you're pitching a film, a product, or your own story, this book is your masterclass in winning people over—without ever throwing a punch."

—Cynthia Rothrock

MARTIAL ARTS LEGEND & ACTION FILM ICON

"The right words, when spoken with the right intention, have the power to transform your entire life. That's exactly what Forbes Riley unlocks in *Pitch Secrets A to Z*. This isn't just another book—it's a proven playbook to help you communicate with clarity, confidence, and conviction so you can create the life you've always dreamed of."

—David Meltzer

CHAIRMAN OF THE NAPOLEON HILL INSTITUTE, ENTREPRENEUR, & INVESTOR

"I've spent my life alongside the greatest motivator I ever knew: my husband, Jack LaLanne. In all those years, I've met few people with that same fire. Forbes Riley is one of them! She doesn't just teach you how to pitch; she inspires you to believe in yourself, to stand tall, and to never quit. *Pitch Secrets A to Z* carries her heart, her wisdom, and her unstoppable energy on every page. You will be motivated, stimulated, and escalated to where you want to be. Jack would have loved this book—and I do too."

THE FIRST LADY OF FITNESS & WELLNESS PIONEER

"In fitness, I've built a career on helping people reach their peak potential. In business, Forbes Riley does the same—showing you how to flex your influence and perfect your pitch. *Pitch Secrets A to Z* is where clarity meets confidence, and Forbes is the ultimate coach."

—Greg Justice

BESTSELLING AUTHOR, FITNESS PIONEER, & HALL OF FAME INDUCTEE

"Forbes Riley's *Pitch Secrets A to Z* is more than a guide to communication — it's a masterclass in energy alignment. With her unique wisdom, she shows you how to direct your influence with clarity and purpose, so your message resonates, your goals align, and abundance flows naturally into your life."

—Marie Diamond

STAR FROM *THE SECRET* & INTERNATIONAL BESTSELLING AUTHOR

"I've co-hosted numerous infomercials with Forbes Riley over the years, and the best way I know to describe her is a 'force of nature.' She is fully invested in every project and wants it to be the very best. Forbes has decades of experience pitching every type of product and service out there, so it's a must-read to learn her proven secrets to success."

—Tom Jourden

AWARD-WINNING INFOMERCIAL HOST & ON-AIR SPOKESPERSON

"I had the pleasure of co-hosting a pitch competition with Forbes Riley, and what I saw was pure mastery. Her ability to draw out the heart of a message and elevate a pitch in real-time is extraordinary. *Pitch Secrets A to Z* is like having Forbes in your corner, teaching you how to communicate with clarity, confidence, and power. This book is a game-changer for anyone serious about being heard."

—Jeff Hoffman

GLOBAL ENTREPRENEUR, PHILANTHROPIST,
& CO-FOUNDER OF PRICELINE.COM

Pitch Secrets A to Z

How to Increase YOUR Influence, Impact & Income

DR. FORBES RILEY
"THE QUEEN OF PITCH"

How to Increase YOUR Influence, Impact & Income

For more information, please contact:
The Forbes Factor
3158 24th Ave. N
St. Petersburg, FL 33713
Media@TheForbesFactor.com

Cover photo credited to: Ann Landstrom

Ordering information for quantity sales: Special discounts are available on quantity purchases by corporations, associations, and others. For details, contact The Forbes Factor at the above address. Programs, products, or services provided by the author are found by contacting them directly. Resources named in the book are found in the resources pages at the back of the book.

Author details: Dr. Forbes Riley, www.ForbesRiley.com
For questions, contact Support@teamforbesriley.com

To book author Dr. Forbes Riley to speak at an event or podcast, please contact Media@TheForbesFactor.com

Library of Congress Control Number: 2025925977
CPSIA Code: PRV0326A
First Edition
ISBN: 979-8-9871293-4-0

Printed in the United States

This book is dedicated to every dreamer, entrepreneur, and inventor (like my dad) who wished they understood how to get their product, service, or ideas out to the world... but never did...

until NOW!

CONTENTS

Increase YOUR Influence, Impact and Income Without Sounding Salesy

SPECIAL FREE BONUS FOR YOU!

Gain Exclusive Access to Scripts, Templates & Tools to Master Your Pitch

Unlock the Free Resource Center

www.PitchSecretsResources.com

Plus, Forbes Riley shares behind the scenes footage and more...

FOREWORD

by Kevin Harrington

Original Shark on *Shark Tank*

When I first met Forbes Riley, I knew she was an accomplished actress, as I had seen her on television and in movies before. Yet, what I didn't know when I was introduced to her was that she was an even more accomplished presenter and powerful *pitch queen*. Her outstanding skills came as a surprise because, if you think about it, not many television personalities are equally talented in the world of pitching or selling. I remember how impressed I was from the first moment I met her; she radiated confidence and spoke eloquently. That day was the beginning of our lifelong friendship and my experience learning how to pitch the "Forbes Riley way." At one point, Forbes and her entire family lived in my guest house when they moved to Florida—those were wonderful times, and the memories we created have been cherished in our family chronicles ever since then.

Today, when Forbes and I spend time together, as we live only a few blocks away from one another in St. Petersburg, Florida, we often talk about how pitching is a largely misunderstood art form. While many believe pitching can be a "negative thing," most simply don't understand how to do it properly. The bad reputation and the lack of skills around pitching are often intertwined. Pitching requires appreciation, skills, and practice. It has sequential elements that need to be presented in the correct order. For example, you need to bring up the problem you are solving before the benefits of your product, followed by the social proof that you have. Pitching has nuances and pacing that make it effective, and few have mastered it the way Forbes ultimately has.

When I was one of the first investors on the hit TV show *Shark Tank*, we often sat on the set, shooting one episode after another for six hours or more. I must tell you, a pitch had to get our attention by being concise and compelling for even the slightest chance of us investing in it. You would be surprised how many of those candidates had neither the skill nor the ability to deliver a winning pitch. This is why it excites me that this book is now available to everyone who wants to master their pitching skills, stand out, and succeed in selling and presenting this way.

Pitching a weak or lackluster closing is one of my pet peeves, and I'm glad to see that Forbes dedicated an entire chapter to it with the letter "C" Closing: Sealing the Deal with Confidence. Even the most brilliant pitch is worthless if you do not close the deal at the end.

When I first started pitching products, I watched guys like Billy Mays and Arnold Morris pitch repeatedly. Do you know what I found? Those guys, who are the rock stars of product sales, barely change anything about their pitch—once they see what works, they double down on those elements and master the order of introducing every part of the pitch, including the jokes, reference stories, and "trial closes," another term you're about to learn.

Most importantly, they use a very powerful technique, which Forbes will explain, to connect with and close people at the end of their pitch, ensuring thousands of yeses and tremendous success.

I am happy to attest that what Forbes offers in *Pitch Secrets A to Z* is priceless. She shares the exact tools she has collected and perfected over decades, giving you everything you need to build your perfect pitch. If you follow her steps and use the tools she provides, you will soon master the technique and be on your way to creating a winning pitch and closing every sale.

I can say this with confidence and affection: Forbes Riley is truly the queen of pitch, crowned by her skills and exceptional ability to help others master the art of pitching. Her dedication to this craft and her desire to share these attributes with you will be what you need to confidently navigate any "shark tank" and emerge triumphant.

Embrace the process she shares and find yourself making better deals, succeeding more often, and enjoying yourself.

Pitching is an art form, and when you master it, both Forbes and I agree, you'll experience outstanding results that will transform and elevate your entire life.

Kevin Harrington

PREFACE

Growing up, my world went silent at 8 years old.

The orthodontist didn't just give me braces—he transformed my mouth into an engineering project, complete with headgear, a tongue thruster, and rubber bands. For 2 years, my words were trapped behind metal, and no one could understand a thing I said. Imagine—a chatty 8-year-old girl, suddenly robbed of her voice.

But sometimes, our greatest struggles give birth to our greatest gifts.

In those 2 years of forced silence, I developed a superpower: the ability to truly see and hear how people really communicate. While my classmates rambled without impact and teachers struggled to hold attention, I sat quietly, decoding the secret language of human connection. I watched parents miss moments to bond with their kids, friends fumble chances to support each other, and adults talk past one another in an endless dance of misunderstanding.

I didn't realize it at 8 years old, but looking back, it's clear why those silent years set me on the path I'm on today.

Communication isn't about how much you say; it's about the impact of what you say. Being unable to speak gave me a profound understanding of clarity, brevity, and connection.

That lesson became the foundation for everything I do, and it's how I became known as the *Queen of Pitch*. As I regained my voice, I was determined not just to speak but to connect, move, inspire, and motivate people with my words. That journey led me to stages, TV screens, and boardrooms, where I've pitched products that generated over $2.5 Billion in sales. But more than that, it led me to transform lives through the power of pitching and effective communication.

Here's what might surprise you: the most valuable pitch isn't the one that closes a million-dollar deal. It's the one that gets your teenager to open up about their day. It's the one that turns your dream job into reality or makes someone believe in your vision. That's the true power of pitching.

That's why I wrote *Pitch Secrets A to Z.*

This isn't just another business book about selling techniques; it's your guide to mastering the single most important skill in life: communicating in a way that moves people to action. Whether you're an entrepreneur growing your business, a professional advancing your career, or a parent building deeper connections, this book will transform how you communicate.

Through 26 proven strategies—one for each letter of the alphabet—you'll learn how to:

- Turn everyday conversations into opportunities
- Speak with confidence and clarity in any situation
- Get your ideas heard and implemented
- Build deeper connections that last
- Transform your message into meaningful results

Each chapter, from A for Attitude to Z for Zoom, unlocks a new level of your communication potential. This isn't about memorizing scripts or using manipulative tactics. It's about mastering the art of authentic human connection—a skill that will serve you in every area of your life.

Whether you're pitching to investors, presenting to your team, or having dinner with your family, these strategies will help you communicate more effectively and persuasively. I've used these exact techniques to build multiple successful businesses, close billions in sales, and create lasting relationships both personally and professionally.

Your voice matters. Your ideas matter. And most importantly, the way you share them matters.

Welcome to *Pitch Secrets A to Z*. Let's transform not just how you communicate, but how you connect, influence, and achieve your dreams.

THE POWER OF THE PITCH

Before we dive head in, I want to delight and inspire you by sharing some of my proudest accomplishments, captured in photos and stories that demonstrate the true impact of a powerful pitch.

These moments remind me that when you wholeheartedly believe in your mission and what you're pitching, magic happens. When you communicate that belief with passion and purpose, there's no limit to what you can achieve. I share these snapshots of my journey not just to tell my story, but to show you the limitless potential within yourself. Get ready to discover the extraordinary possibilities that unfold when you unlock the secrets and master the art of pitching.

Let's begin with a single pitch that grossed $1 Billion, the Jack LaLanne Power Juicer, which became one of the most successful infomercials of ALL TIME.

Jack LaLanne

He wasn't just a fitness legend—he was one of my greatest mentors, alongside his incredible wife, Elaine. He pioneered health clubs, invented the leg extension machine, and hosted the first-ever fitness TV series on air for an astounding 34 years. But what truly set him apart was his unwavering passion and conviction to help people get healthy. For Jack, pitching wasn't about selling; it was about sharing his life's mission.

His motto, "It's not what you do some of the time that counts; it's what you do all of the time that counts," became my guiding principle. Jack's boundless energy, storytelling, and purpose changed my life and millions of others'. I've included a special clip on the Resource Center so you can witness his magic firsthand.

This photo shows my twins, Ryker and Makenna, absorbing Jack's wisdom of his famous advice, *"If man made it, don't eat it!"* Today, they've grown into fit, health-conscious individuals, proving that great mentors shape lives. Jack and Elaine set the gold standard for pitching with purpose and living fully. But he was just the beginning of my success journey.

Anthony "Sully" Sullivan

We shared some incredible moments in the world of infomercials, including the launch of Soda Club and later SpinGym on his hit show on Discovery Channel, *PitchMen*. As the force behind OxiClean and Swivel Sweeper, he knows how to take a product and generate millions with his quick wit and magnetic presence. In this photo I had won *Best Product* on Home Shopping for SpinGym and *Best Celebrity TV Host*, truly a full-circle moment. I'll never forget his words: *"With the Juicer, Forbes had one of the biggest monster successes ever, and if you want a girl to sell your product, SHE is your go-to girl!"*

Billy Mays

Like a force of nature, with his booming voice and unmatched energy, Billy turned everyday products into household names. His signature "Hi, Billy Mays here!" opened millions of wallets and revolutionized direct response advertising. Along with Sully, he helped launch my fitness invention, SpinGym, on their Discovery reality show *PitchMen*—a dream come true. Here we are reviewing scripts, bringing ideas to life with Billy's magic touch. Want to see how our journey unfolded? Check out the full episode on our Resource Center.

Jake "Body by Jake" Steinfeld

This photo captures a career-defining moment with Body by Jake (Jake Steinfeld), the first personal trainer to the stars. I met Jake while auditioning for his new network, Cable Health Club (later FitTV). He asked me to "pitch a pen," sparking a partnership that led us to pitch over 1,500 health and fitness products together. His mentorship shaped my career, and in 1995, he sold the network to Fox for $500 million. Working with Jake laid the foundation for everything I've built since.

Kim Kardashian

Few people know that one of Kim Kardashian's earliest TV appearances was in a Steam Iron infomercial with me! Head to the Resource Center to watch it. In 2006, before the Kardashians were a household name, Kim was organizing closets, selling celebrity clothes on eBay, and had just opened her first store, *Dash*. She flew to Florida, and together, we pitched this product. We had a great time, and it's a moment I'll always cherish. Watching her journey from there has been remarkable—the rest, as they say, is history.

Les Brown

Not only one of the greatest motivational speakers in the world—he's also one of my dearest friends and mentors. With his smooth voice and mastery of language, Les is one of the greatest pitchers EVER. Watching him captivate audiences and inspire action has been a masterclass in the art of communication. His famous line *"You gotta be hungry!"* speaks volumes about the passion and persistence he brings to everything he does. Having the privilege to learn from him and call him a friend has been one of the greatest gifts in my journey.

Mario Lopez

He may have started as a teenage heartthrob playing A.C. Slater on the hit TV series *Saved by the Bell*, but he's grown into so much more as a dynamic TV host, and, yes, a truly great pitchman. His passion for fitness made him the ideal co-host for the innovative product we collaborated on, and working alongside him was pure joy. His warm, welcoming smile makes you feel like *you* are the most important person in the room. That's the magic of Mario—he lifts others as he shines.

Montel Williams

He was a talk show icon I admired for years, so getting to co-host 3 infomercials with him, including the $800M HealthMaster Blender, was nothing short of surreal. What surprised me most? He was a fan of mine, too. Our on-camera chemistry was pure magic, but it was his strength and grace, facing MS while spreading a message of health and hope, that truly inspired me. Forever a fan of his heart, his hustle, and his unstoppable spirit. Some people host shows; Montel *changed lives*.

Richard Simmons

The beloved fitness icon behind *Sweatin' to the Oldies* made fitness fun and accessible for millions. His unique pitching style was so relatable and authentic that it resonated with everyone, whether on QVC, where we both appeared, or through his groundbreaking workout programs. As fellow inductees in the Fitness Hall of Fame, I've learned so much from Richard, especially how to connect with people on a deeper level through passion and sincerity. His ability to make everyone feel seen and valued has had a lasting impact on me.

Serena Williams

Contrary to popular belief, I did not beat Serena in a tennis match. But we have gone head to head when it comes to pitching—she still won. With the heart and spirit of a true champion, we sold Mission Cool Towels on HSN, and yes, she loves my SpinGym! The biggest lesson I learned from this rock star is that everyone needs a coach to succeed, no matter how good you are. You also need to practice. In fact, I have a chapter devoted to practice; thanks, Serena!

Tony Horton

Before P90X became a global sensation, I had the honor of working with Tony Horton on Power 90. From day one, Tony brought unmatched passion, discipline, and charisma to everything he did. What struck me most was his ability to lead with authenticity and ignite transformation not just in the body—but in the mind. That early collaboration taught me the power of presence on camera and the importance of showing up with energy and belief in what you're sharing. I'm forever grateful for what I learned beside him, and proud to have been a small part of his iconic fitness legacy.

Tony Little

An unstoppable force in the world of fitness—Tony's energy, resilience, and signature ponytail made him a household name. From our collaborations on the infomercial for Pure Protein to our time at HSN, I've seen firsthand how his infectious positivity and entrepreneurial spirit inspired millions. His famous line, *"You can do it,"* is more than just a catchphrase; it's a way of life. Tony's drive to help others succeed makes him a true role model in fitness, business, and life.

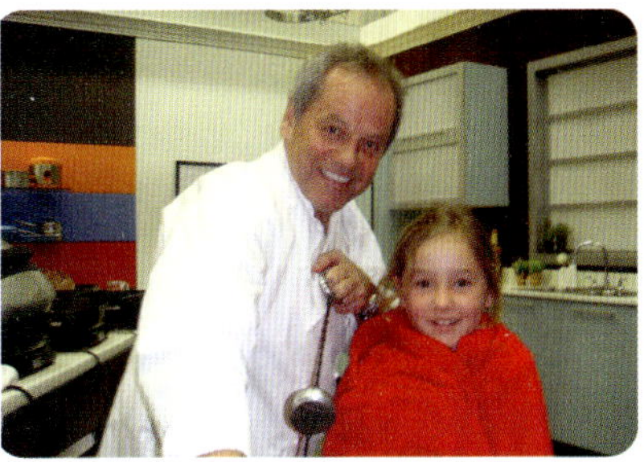

Wolfgang Puck and I worked together on HSN, and it wasn't just about cooking. Wolf couldn't resist playing with my fitness products, from the SpinGym to jumping on the Rebounder. Hanging out in the kitchen with him and my daughter, Makenna, we got to enjoy his culinary expertise and playful spontaneity.

Along the way, I won Awards for Pitching!

Over the years, I've had the honor of winning multiple awards at the ERA (Electronic Retailing Association) annual event, often called the "Oscars of Infomercials."

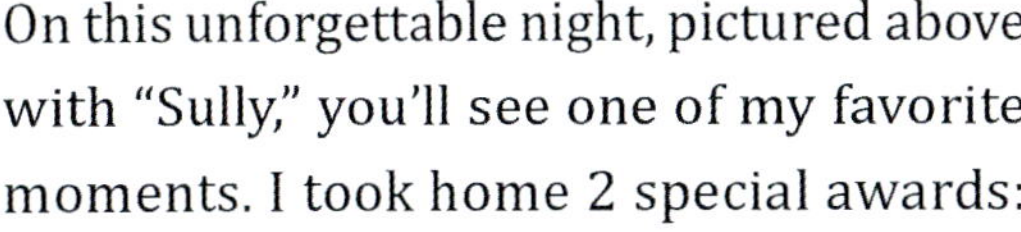

On this unforgettable night, pictured above with "Sully," you'll see one of my favorite moments. I took home 2 special awards: Best Female Presenter of the Year for the fifth time plus Best Live Home Shopping Guest of the Year, for my work with SpinGym. *What a ride!*

Here I am co-hosting with senior Guthy-Renker executive Elliot Segal.

The event was filled with excitement—until my high heels had a mind of their own on the way up the stairs to accept the award.

Let's just say it made for a moment (and a video) well worth watching!

This plaque was awarded by Clickfunnels founder, Russell Brunson, to my business partner and daughter, Makenna Riley, and me for successfully generating $1 Million dollars from a single marketing funnel—earning us a place in the prestigious "2 Comma Club."

This milestone celebrates the incredible journey of our online Pitching Community and the impact we've made together. As of the printing of this book, our company has just surpassed 100,000 students.

One of the greatest honors of my life...

was receiving an honorary Doctorate in Business and the Presidential Lifetime Achievement Award— not for fame or fortune, but for dedicating my life to empowering others.

It reminds me that every pitch I've given, every student I've mentored, and every stage I've stepped onto was part of a much bigger mission: to help people believe in themselves, own their voice, and turn their ideas into impact.

I didn't set out to win awards; I set out to make a difference. This recognition simply affirmed that I'm on the right path.

These aren't just accolades—they're milestones in a journey fueled by passion, authenticity, and a bit of pitch-perfect magic. From fitness gadgets to beauty breakthroughs, I've helped turn great ideas into household names, pioneered an industry, and redefined the way the world shops and sells.

Every time I walk past the trophy case in my TV studio, I'm reminded of what's possible when you master the art of the pitch. Over the years, I've been honored:

- 🏆 7x Best Female Presenter of the Year
- 🏆 2x Best Live Home Shopping Guest
- 🏆 Best Infomercial Product of the Year
- 🏆 Best Infomercial of the Year
- 🏆 Best Author & Coach Influencer

Want to see the evolution of my infomercials, TV history, and live pitch magic in action?

Scan the QR Code or visit the link to unlock behind-the-scenes footage, legendary product demos, rare broadcast clips, and FREE bonus content from *Pitch Secrets A to Z.*

www.PitchSecretsResources.com

Here Are a Few of the Infomercials I've Appeared In...

Ab & Thigh Roller
Ab Rocker
Abs of Steel
Absolo
Abtronics
Advacal
Aerobed
AgeFit Skin Cream
Air Press Massage Boots
Alps Printer
Anthony Morrison Books
Aqua Clean Wet & Dry Vac
Aroma-Trim
Best of All Malls
Biodepolis
BioForm
Bionic Ear with Lee Majors
Body Rider
Buckwheat Pillow
Budget Blinds
Bumpits
Bun & Thigh Isolator
Buns of Steel
Butt Burner
Bye-bye Babyfat
Cami Secret
CBD Pain Relief
Chiptastic
Clear Glow Detox Mask
Comet Skin Cream
Commodities & You
Covert Bailey
Creations in Minutes
Crisp Wave Air Grill
Decorate Like a Pro
Delete Cleaner
Derma Renew Glow
Dirt BeGone

Doggone Groom Solutions
Down Around Pillow
Dust Defender Max
Dust Vortex Pro
Dr. Brooks Foot Insoles
Dr. Ordon Rejuvenation
Dual Trainer
Easy Design Pro
Eat Journal
ediets.com
Elliptical Cycle
Epiclear
Exerflex
Facebook Ad—
Adrian Morrison
Fem Free
Flex Fusion Core Roller
FlexTone Bands
Fluidity Bar
Forbes Flawless Skin Care
Fresh Wave Mist
Froth Wave Coffee Maker
Fun With Phonics
Government Grants
Gone in 60 Secs Eye Serum
GymFlex
Gym in a Box
Gyro Trainer
HealthMaster with Montel
HealthMaster 100
Health Pak
Home-based Business
Honeywell Clean Air
Hooked on Phonics
HydraWrap Nail Mask
Hydroderm
I Mobile Tech Hub
Infrared Grill

Insta Art Nail Stamp Kit
Instant Cooker Stove Top
Instant Photo Fix
Instyler Rotating Iron
Irwin Naturals
Jack LaLanne Juicer
Jack LaLanne Juicer Express
Laser Eye
Life Force 200
Life Imaging Heart Scan
Knee Pain Eraser
Mattress Topper
MaxiClimber
Maxiglide Hair Straightener
Micro Grill
Microradiant Cooker
Mind Mapping
More Furniture for Less
Natural Solutions
Neuropathy Pain Relief
NutriGrill
OmniClick
Orbital 360
Orbitrek
Oriental Trading Craft Box
Paint Mate by Wagner
Peak Performance
Phil Up and Go
Pilates 101
Power 90
Power Air Fryer
Power Chopper
Power Cooker
Power Plate Pro
Power Pro Pilates
Power Pulse Bar
Power Reader Eyeglasses
Power Sweep X-1

But wait, there's more!

- Pressa Bella Steam Iron
- Profile Toner
- Prostrong Nails
- Pure Protein with Tony Little
- Pure Radiance Elixir
- QMI Oil Additive
- Quantum Nutrition
- Quick Step Cardio Pad
- Quick Fix Nail Serum
- Radiant Eye Lift Serum
- Rainbow Steamer
- Rapid Hair Growth
- Real Estate Solutions
- Real Estate—Cody Sperber
- Red Skelton Comedy
- Restore & More
- Robert Irvine Cookware
- Ronco Dehydrator
- Ronco Rotisserie
- Sensa Weight Loss
- Simply Postage
- Silver Secret
- SlamMan Puncher

- Slice Master Pro
- Slimming Pants
- Smart Chopper
- Soapworks
- Social Media Profits
- Soda Machine
- Solutions USA
- Sonic Vac
- Sonoma Express
- Sparkle: Pro Surface Cleaner
- SpinGym
- Spiritual Cinema
- Sports Care Pain Relief
- Stain Away Boost
- Steam Iron
- Steam Max
- Stem Cell Neuropathy
- Stem Cell Teeth Whitener
- Success TV
- The O Ring
- Thermage Laser
- Toastmaster Supreme
- Total Chef University
- Total Gym

- Top Chef University
- Travel Savers
- TriGeniX vitamins
- TurboBlender
- TV Shop
- U Define U
- Urban Rebounder
- Ultimate Love Songs
- Ultraflex
- US Search
- Vacation Voyages
- VersaClimber
- Vertigrill
- Vitala-trim
- Vital Boost Hair Serum
- Wizetrade
- Wrinkle Be Gone
- X-Factor Multi Styler
- You Gotta Hungry—Les Brown
- Zach & Dani's Coffee Roaster
- Z Mei skin care line
- Zoobooks

INTRODUCTION

Mastering the Pitch from A to Z

"3... 2... 1... You're live on QVC!"

In that instant, the cameras roll, the lights flood the stage, and I step into the moment. Somewhere out there, a woman in her pajamas is flipping through channels at 3:00 a.m., not looking to buy anything—just unwinding after a long day. She's not waiting, credit card in hand, ready to be sold. She's simply watching.

But in the next few minutes, it's my job to change that.

Not by pushing a product, but by telling a story, by creating a connection and turning skepticism into belief. If I do my job right, she won't just see another sales pitch—she'll see *herself* in the experience I'm creating. And when that moment happens, she won't think twice. She'll pick up the phone, make the call, and transform from a passive viewer into an engaged buyer.

That's the power of the pitch.

When the numbers finally rolled in, my pitch had been a raging success. And I wasn't just invited back to QVC; I became a staple on home shopping channels globally for over 30 years, generating millions in sales, not by chance, but by design.

You see, the success wasn't luck. It was the result of mastering a formula, a blend of art and science that turns an ordinary sales pitch into a magnetic moment of truth. Over the decades, I refined this formula, turning everyday features into irresistible benefits, casual viewers into loyal customers, and simple ideas into million-dollar realities.

But here's the truth: the power of the pitch isn't just reserved for TV screens and sales floors. It's everywhere.

In today's world your ability to pitch effectively matters more than ever. We live in a world full of distractions, short attention spans, and endless competition. If you can't capture and hold someone's attention quickly, you risk getting overlooked.

Pitching isn't just a sales tactic—it's a superpower.

Your ability to pitch influences every area of your life: getting a job, landing a promotion, buying a home, even persuading someone to say *yes* to a first date.

You're already pitching every single day. Every time you introduce yourself, ask for an opportunity, or share an idea, you're making a pitch. The question is: Are you doing it effectively?

This book will teach you how to communicate with precision, confidence, and success, whether you're pitching your business, your brand, or yourself.

So, you might ask, who is this book right for?

The **real estate agent** who turns a hesitant buyer into a homeowner.

The **job seeker** who walks into an interview and leaves with an offer.

The **nonprofit leader** who inspires donors to fund their mission.

The **athlete** looking to secure their first major sponsorship deal.

The **author** who gets a publisher to take a chance on their book.

The **salesperson** who transforms a cold lead into a lifelong customer.

The **coach** who rallies their team to believe in themselves and win.

The **aspiring influencer** who lands their first brand collaboration.

The **entrepreneur** who lands the funding after countless rejections.

The **startup founder** who turns an idea into a movement.

Here's what might surprise you: the most valuable pitch isn't just the one that closes a million-dollar deal. It's the person getting down on one knee, asking the love of their life to say yes. It's the parent who has managed to get their entire family to do their chores, consistently. It's the teacher who turns an uninterested student into a lifelong learner.

That's the true power of pitching. It's not just about business; it's about getting people to listen, believe, and take action.

No matter who you are, where you work, or what you do, **you are pitching every single day**.

If you're not seeing the results you want, it's not because your ideas aren't good enough or your passion isn't strong enough—it's because you haven't been taught how to communicate them in a way that makes people say yes.

How to Use This Book

This isn't your typical business book filled with high-level theories and 30,000-foot overviews. *Pitch Secrets A to Z* is a hands-on, results-driven experience designed to sharpen your communication and master the art of pitching in real time.

Every chapter is a teaching moment, packed with tools you can use immediately. Whether you're an entrepreneur selling a product, a professional negotiating a deal, or simply someone who wants to articulate your value more powerfully, you'll find a step-by-step framework to help you pitch with confidence and clarity.

Together, they form your complete pitch toolkit—delivering proven strategies, practical tips, personal insights, and scripts pulled straight from my journey as *The Queen of Pitch*. These lessons work just as powerfully in boardrooms and sales calls as they do in chance conversations, interviews, and everyday life.

Here’s a sneak peek at what awaits:

- **A is for Attitude**: Unlock 7 powerful techniques to boost your confidence and command any room you walk into.
- **B is for Belief:** Break free from the mental blocks and limiting stories that have kept you playing small.
- **C is for Closing**: Master the art of closing deals authentically without feeling pushy or salesy
- And ending with...
- **Z is for Zoom**: Master the art of virtual presence so you can pitch, connect, and convert in the digital world.

Each letter holds a key. Each chapter, a breakthrough. Whether you’re pitching to investors, negotiating a deal, or simply introducing yourself at a dinner party, *Pitch Secrets A to Z* is your ultimate guide to turning every conversation into an opportunity.

Why Now?

There comes a moment in every person’s life when a pitch makes the difference between success and rejection. Whether you realize it or not, you’re always pitching. Every time you ask for something, introduce yourself, or propose an idea, you’re pitching. This book will show you how to do it with precision, confidence, and success.

So here’s *my* pitch to you:

Let’s unlock your full potential together. Inside *Pitch Secrets A to Z*, you’ll gain the mindset, knowledge, and strategies to transform your communication and, by extension, your life.

To your success,

Forbes Riley

P.S. To get the most out of this journey, we've created an interactive Resource Center that brings each chapter to life and helps you apply what you learn immediately. Simply scan the QR Code to dive deeper.

→ Watch exclusive video lessons that expand on each concept.

→ Access ready-to-use templates, tools, and pitch-building materials.

→ Get instant links to resources, websites, and insider tips mentioned in the book.

These bonus materials are designed to accelerate your progress, deepen your mastery, and help you start seeing results—*fast*.

Don't just read the book—*experience* it.

"Be willing to do what others are not willing to do, to get things that others only dream of."

—Les Brown

CHAPTER A: Attitude

Attitude (noun): *The unspoken energy behind every pitch—it's the confidence, conviction, and presence you project before you ever say a word.*

Are you picking up this book because you think you're not good at pitching—or believe you're just not a "natural" at selling? Think again. It's not a flaw; it's simply a skill you haven't learned yet—and that's exactly what's about to change. You just haven't yet acquired the tools to become a master of your pitch. Attitude is the mindset and energy you bring into every pitch, conversation, and opportunity. With clarity comes confidence and this book is your roadmap to turn what might feel like a mess into a magnetic, meaningful message. You're not far off. In fact, you're closer than you think. Let's flip the switch and unlock the power of your pitch.

The first step to nailing your pitch? Realizing that your **attitude speaks louder than your words.** Pitching isn't just about what you say—it's how you show up. Your facial expressions, posture, tone, and energy all deliver a message before you ever open your mouth.

People notice your attitude the moment you step into a room or appear on a Zoom screen. If you're feeling defeated, unsure, or disempowered, it impacts your audience more than any words ever could. To set the right tone, start with a positive mindset, practice uplifting self-talk, and let your enthusiasm shine through your presence and demeanor.

This killer combination will help you to effectively pitch any product, service, or idea.

I learned this the hard way. Early in my acting career, I was fortunate enough to study in Los Angeles, under Academy Award–winning film director Milton Katselas. He drilled 5 core lessons into all his students, truths that have guided me through every stage of my life and still shape how I show up today.

"Energy is Everything." What you bring into the room is what people remember most. Your words matter, but your energy sticks.

"You are the Message." People don't just buy what you're selling—they buy you. Your passion, your presence, your purpose, so don't wait to be chosen. Choose yourself.

"90% of Success is Just Showing Up." Opportunity doesn't chase perfection—it rewards those who consistently show up, ready or not, with heart and hustle.

"It's YOUR Responsibility to Turn Your Dreams into Action." No one's coming to rescue your dream—it's on you to take the first step and keep stepping, even when the path isn't clear.

"Attitude Monitors Talent." Talent may get attention, but it's your attitude that earns trust, builds connection, and keeps you in the room.

The last comment hit me the hardest: **"Attitude monitors talent."** Milton used to say that attitude shapes your internal beliefs, which become actions—and those actions spark either positive or negative reactions from the world around you. He often used this phrase to explain why less talented actors were consistently cast in major roles, while others with more skill faded into obscurity. The truth? No one wants to deal with negativity—not on a film set, not in a boardroom, not in a friendship, and certainly not in love. Talent might open the door, but attitude is what keeps it open.

If you've got a bad attitude, it doesn't matter how talented you are... at some point, people will no longer want to work with you.

Milton would say, "When all is crushing your spirit... just smile. Smile until your cheeks hurt and watch how others will smile back. In your darkest moment, let your teeth shine bright." Funny enough, that is one of my secrets to success.

When it comes to having a successful pitch, it starts with personal clarity. If you are stressed out and solely focused on making sales, your pitch begins to sound desperate, your energy feels harsh, and you're bound to face rejection.

With clarity comes the ability to be empathetic, overcome failure with ease, and nurture a healthy mindset. The key to finding personal clarity begins with:

- Your Morning Routine and Daily Habit
- Fostering a Sense of Gratitude
- A Clutter-Free Environment
- Establishing a "Why" Bigger Than Money
- Cultivating Healthy Relationships
- Joining a Supportive Community—Being Part of Something Bigger Than Yourself

An understanding of these actions and daily practice will result in a mindset shift and allow you to not only nail the "perfect pitch," but evolve into the ideal pitcher. You'll become someone who can easily go from pitching a product or service, to a charity event, or enrolling investors to raise millions of dollars. However, even with a mindset shift, how do you create a positive pitch attitude?

7 CREATIVE WAYS TO BUILD YOUR PPA (POSITIVE PITCH ATTITUDE)

...even when you're having a bad day

How do you keep your positive pitch attitude when life isn't going your way? These strategies will help you stay confident, focused, and pitch-ready—no matter what the day throws at you:

1. **Mirror, Mirror, on the Wall**
   Look yourself in the eye and deliver your pitch like you're talking to your future self who's already made it. This isn't about ego—it's about belief. See the version of you who's already won. Step up to a mirror (your car rear view, a handheld, or simply go to the bathroom), look yourself in the eyes, and say out loud: "I am a powerhouse. I am confident. I OWN this pitch!" The energy you bring is contagious, so if you don't believe in yourself, why would anyone else? Practice pitching to yourself daily—it's not vanity, it's victory in the making!

2. **Dress Like Your Future Self**
   Your pitch starts *before* you open your mouth. So suit up—like the 6 or 7-figure version of yourself. When you look good, you feel unstoppable. When you feel unstoppable, you pitch with purpose and power.

3. **The Gratitude Flip**
   Feeling nervous? Stuck in your head? Here's the trick: Flip it with gratitude! Before you pitch, take 60 seconds to write down 3 things you're thankful for: your health, your hustle, your why. This practice rewires your energy, creates a positive vibe, and makes you magnetic to your audience.

4. **Create a "Power Playlist"**

   Music is fuel. Build a playlist of songs that instantly shift your vibe—victory anthems, boss energy, and tracks that remind you who you are. THEN MOVE! Yes, I said it! Move your body before you move your mouth. Dance around the room, jump, shake it off—whatever gets your blood pumping and those endorphins flowing. When you're physically energized, you project confidence like nobody's business. (One of my mood-shifting songs is "I Love Me" by Meghan Trainor.)

5. **Visualize the YES**

   Close your eyes. Picture your audience leaning in, nodding, and saying, *"Wow, I love this!"* Visualize the moment they say *YES* to your offer, and anchor yourself in that feeling. When you see it, feel it, and believe it, you create it.

6. **Mind Your Small Talk**

   Don't lead with how bad your day's been. Save the dog drama, the near car crash, or the sick kids for later. Small talk before a pitch is *prime time* to build rapport. Even if you're off your game, fake the sunshine. Compliment their necklace. Share a light moment. Keep it bright and connected. People buy energy—make yours worth investing in. Leave the "whine" for the dinner table and bring your best energy to the conversation!

7. **Stop Letting the Perfect Ruin the Good**

   Waiting for the perfect pitch? Don't. Progress beats perfection every time. If it's not flowing, *adjust and keep going*. Even if today's pitch doesn't land, plant the seed for tomorrow's yes. As Wayne Gretzky says, "You miss 100% of the shots you don't take."

Attitude isn't just a mindset; it's a lifestyle, one that shines through in every pitch and every interaction. A Positive Pitch Attitude (PPA) is your secret weapon, the edge that sets you apart. Even on your toughest days, PPA can keep you grounded and effective. It's not about pretending everything is perfect; it's about standing tall, owning your voice, and pitching anyway.

I've witnessed the transformation and now, it's your turn. Your attitude is your foundation, your gateway to the future you dream of, and the cornerstone of building your million-dollar pitch.

For those days when you need an extra boost, I created a *free 7-Day Motivational Video Series* just for you. Each short, powerful video is designed to help you strengthen your *Positive Pitch Attitude*, so you stay empowered and focused.

Remember, when you lead with a POSITIVE attitude, the world starts saying "YES." Let's pitch like your future depends on it, because it does.

Scan the QR Code to unlock the Video Series and other free materials inside the Resource Center (Chapter A).

Let's jump-start your journey to building momentum today.

"We've been lying to ourselves because it's hard to believe that we are as extraordinary as we are."
—Forbes Riley

CHAPTER B: Belief

Belief (noun): *A trust, faith, or confidence in someone or something that shapes thoughts, actions, and outcomes even without absolute proof.*

Belief is more than a mindset; it's your unshakable foundation for success. It powers your pitch, transforms doubts into confidence, and turns hesitation into action. When you combine belief with practice and momentum, you create a force so magnetic that others can't help but say "YES." Remember, the success of your pitch and your life starts with believing in yourself first. So stand tall, speak boldly, and pitch with the conviction that your vision deserves. The future is yours to create!

If you don't fully believe in who you are and what you're offering, how can you expect anyone else to?

The truth is, people can sense your energy long before they even hear your words. The conviction behind your message, your unwavering belief, has a magnetic quality. It attracts attention, commands respect, and makes your pitch feel authentic. Belief isn't just about confidence or self-assurance; it's about a deeply ingrained mindset. Your belief system is what drives your words, actions, and the energy you project.

Pitch Starts with YOU

Your belief system is like the operating system of your life. If it's running smoothly, everything else follows. If it's full of bugs—doubt, fear, or limiting beliefs—then even the most well-crafted pitch will fall flat. You can learn all the techniques and strategies in the world, but if you don't believe in yourself and what you're pitching, none of it will matter. People don't just buy products—they buy into your certainty, your passion, and your vision for what's possible.

Before you even think about standing in front of an audience, you will want to start by pitching to the most important person in the room—yourself. If you don't believe in yourself, if your inner dialogue is filled with doubt, then your pitch will reflect that insecurity. But when you genuinely believe in yourself and your message, it radiates outward, drawing people in.

Building a Strong Belief System

How do you build a belief system that empowers you to pitch with conviction? It starts with clarity and self-awareness. Here's how:

Define Your Core Values

Your core values shape everything you do. Knowing what you stand for helps you align your message with those values. When you're aligned, your pitch feels natural, and people are more likely to trust you.

Your core values are the principles that guide your decisions and actions. To identify yours, ask: What motivates me? What do I stand for? When you pitch from a place aligned with your values, your message resonates on a deeper level. Some examples of core values:

1. **Integrity**—Being honest and having strong moral principles.
2. **Authenticity**—Staying true to who you are and what you believe.
3. **Passion**—Approaching life and work with energy and enthusiasm.
4. **Growth**—Constantly striving to learn and improve.
5. **Resilience**—Bouncing back from challenges and failures.
6. **Collaboration**—Valuing teamwork and partnerships.

7. **Courage**—Facing fears and taking bold action despite uncertainty.
8. **Excellence**—Striving for the best in everything you do.
9. **Adaptability**—Embracing change and staying flexible in approach.
10. **Generosity**—Giving time, energy, or resources to help others.

Now it's your turn to define your core values.
Begin by choosing 5 that truly reflect who you are. This will form a strong foundation. You can always build on them over time, but start by focusing on what feels most authentic and aligned with your purpose. Take a moment to reflect deeply, uncover what drives you, and list those values below.

My Top 5 Core Values are:

- ______________________________
- ______________________________
- ______________________________
- ______________________________
- ______________________________

Next, we need to get real: belief without action is like having a Ferrari without gas—pretty to look at, but it won't get you anywhere. Your belief system needs more than positive thoughts and vision boards; it needs you to suit up and show up, every single day.

Think of your belief as a muscle. You wouldn't expect to bench-press 200 pounds without training, right? Same goes for your pitch power. Each time you take action, whether it's practicing in front of your bathroom mirror or pitching to a room full of investors—you're doing belief bicep curls.

HERE'S YOUR 3-STEP BELIEF-BUILDING WORKOUT

1. Practice Like You're Getting Featured on the TV Series *Shark Tank*!

Great pitches look effortless for 2 reasons: mastering the right formula and relentless practice. Watch any successful *Shark Tank* entrepreneur—in 60 seconds, they capture attention, demonstrate value, and inspire confidence. This isn't luck or natural talent. It's understanding the structure of a powerful pitch and practicing until it flows like second nature.

This level of mastery doesn't mean memorizing a script. It means understanding your message so deeply that you can adapt it for any audience, answer any question, and handle any curveball with confidence.

When you've internalized both the formula and your message, something remarkable happens: your conviction becomes contagious. Your listener doesn't just hear your words—they feel your passion and want to be part of your vision.

2. Embrace the Uncomfortable

Growth lives outside your comfort zone—that's where breakthroughs happen. Each rejection isn't a stop sign; it's a GPS recalculating your route to success. The more you push past your limits, the more your confidence expands. Every "no" strengthens your journey to "yes." Think of comfort zones like last year's jeans—sometimes you need to outgrow them.

The people who win aren't the ones who *avoid* discomfort; they're the ones who dance with it. When you stumble, sweat, or stumble again—that's your greatness training for game day. Every awkward pitch, every nervous moment on camera, is shaping your power under pressure. Remember, diamonds aren't born in comfort; they're made under pressure and heat. So step into the fire. Growth doesn't just test you . . . it transforms you.

And here's the secret: comfort kills ambition. The second you get too cozy, you stop reaching. Stay curious. Stay hungry. Embrace the uncomfortable. That's where the magic, mastery, and momentum live. Every time you stretch yourself, you expand what's possible and before long, what once scared you becomes your new normal.

3. Turn Action into Momentum

Success isn't about a single dramatic leap—it's the consistent steps you take each day that lead to greatness. Every action creates a ripple effect, building energy and progress.

Start now: send that email, make that call, deliver that pitch. Each step strengthens your belief and fuels the next, creating a powerful cycle of growth and forward motion. What starts small can grow into something unstoppable.

Momentum compounds faster than motivation. Action creates evidence, and evidence builds certainty. Each follow-through shifts you from hoping to knowing. When you move first, confidence follows. Stack small wins daily, and momentum will carry you further than willpower ever could.

A well-practiced pitch backed by genuine belief is like a heat-seeking missile of persuasion and influence. When you combine unshakeable belief with consistent action, success is inevitable. When belief meets action, there are no limits to what you can achieve.

Start today—build your belief, master your pitch, and watch the world say "YES" to your vision. Now, get out there and let's transform opportunities into outcomes.

"I don't sell products—
I provide solutions!"
—Forbes Riley

CHAPTER C: Closing

Closing (noun): *The final stage of a process, transaction, or negotiation where a decision or agreement is confirmed.*

I always find it funny when people say they "hate" closing when they're doing it every single day! Have you ever convinced someone to go to your choice of restaurant, vacation spot, or movie—and they agreed? Congratulations, you just closed a pitch!

You may not realize just how much closing is everywhere in everyday life. If you request a simple favor that might seem small, yet you persuade someone to take on the task, then you've successfully closed the pitch.

Here are some examples:

- Getting a neighbor to water your plants while you're on vacation
- Convincing a friend to join you for an early-morning workout
- Getting a group of friends to try a new game or hobby you love

When you get a series of YESes in a pitch, the close becomes a no-brainer. This concept will amaze you, not only because of the ease of selling your offer, but also how the ease of closing shows up in every aspect of your life.

Pitching as a **life skill** gives you the power to get a YES from anyone you want:

- A room upgrade at a hotel
- Your choice of movie or restaurant
- Getting your child to clean their room
- Your spouse to take out the garbage
- And the ultimate pitch, asking someone to marry you!

Pitching as a **business principle** allows you to:

- Make sales
- Get investors
- Create partnerships
- Get onto talk shows or in magazines
- Raise money
- Attract prospects to your event
- Make effective presentations
- Get a raise from your boss

Closing BEGINS with Getting a YES

In typical "sales," closing usually means an exchange of money. But in pitching your goal is to get a YES. When you stop fixating on making money as the end result, you'll take unnecessary pressure off the conversation.

Here's my secret weapon: I play a game in my head when I'm pitching—collect as many YESes as possible before I go for the close! It's called Trial Closing, and it's pure magic. By the time I ask for the final commitment, it feels like an easy transition because the customer has already been saying yes! This strategy involves getting several small YESes throughout your pitch, leading up to the big one that seals the deal.

To make any close successful, your goal is to get buy-ins throughout the pitch. You want the clients to say yes in their heads before they say yes with their mouth. This isn't about manipulation—it's about creating an environment where your prospect feels comfortable and confident in their decision.

You can incorporate trial closes that are almost guaranteed to get you a YES throughout your pitch by asking these questions:

- "Would you agree it's time to take action and make a change?"
- "You want solutions that work, don't you?"
- "Would you agree it's time to stop settling for less than you deserve?"
- "You want to make a bigger impact, don't you?"
- "This sounds exciting, right?"

These aren't just random questions. They're strategic stepping stones that guide your prospect toward the final close, often without them realizing it. With each "yes" you create momentum, making the final agreement feel natural rather than forced. By steadily building trust throughout the conversation, you're allowing them to see the value of your offer on their terms. This gradual alignment fosters a genuine connection, leading to a close that feels easy, authentic, and mutually beneficial.

I like to say, "Get 3 YESes, and you've got yourself a deal." Why? Because every "yes" builds ownership. By the time you're ready for the final close, your prospect has already agreed with you multiple times, which means that the last "yes" is almost inevitable.

But here's where most people mess up: they wait until the end to handle objections. One of the first steps in crafting your pitch is understanding what objections might come up. When it comes to effectively closing, the secret is NOT to wait until the end of your pitch to handle them.

Your best plan of action? As they used to say in old Western movies, "Head 'em off at the pass!" Or more simply, incorporate possible objections in the body of your pitch before they even come up.

Common objections you may run into include:

• It's too expensive. • I don't have time. • I'm not ready to start now.	• I need to consult my partner. • It's not right for me. • I don't need your product/service.

For example, one evening my 5-year-old son, Ryker, walked into my office around dinnertime and said, "Mom, can I have a piece of candy?" With a little chuckle I responded, "No, it's almost time to eat. Go play." About 5 minutes later my son comes back, looks at me with his big blue eyes, and says, "Mommy, can I have a piece of candy if I promise to eat all my broccoli?" I smiled at his ingenious way to handle objections but still said, "No, dinner will be ready soon." A few minutes later he comes back, stomps his foot and says, "Mom, I'm 5 years old and I just want a piece of candy."

His cuteness wore me down and I said, "Yes." Interestingly enough he didn't come back because he pitched me effectively, and got what he wanted. This begs the question: **Does "no" mean stop or go?** Each time my son got a NO, he continued to hone his pitch, until he got the YES he was looking for.

Let's RE-IMAGINE that the word "NO" stands for:
N—Never-ending
O—Opportunity

Every "no" is a window into your prospect's mind. They're not shutting you down; they're telling you exactly what they need to hear to say "yes." The secret? Weave the answers into your pitch before they even raise the concern. For example, if you know price might be an issue, highlight the return on investment early. If time is a concern, showcase how your solution saves hours before they bring it up. This proactive approach transforms potential roadblocks into stepping stones.

Many people feel anxious about closing because they haven't built enough momentum throughout their pitch. They treat the close like a high-stakes moment instead of the natural next step in a conversation that's been flowing toward "yes" all along.

Trial closes aren't just about getting agreement—they let you gauge interest and address concerns in real time. If someone hesitates on a trial close, that's your chance to adjust course before the final ask. It's the GPS that recalculates your route when you make a wrong turn.

But what about when you've done everything right and still get a "no"? Here's my secret sauce that's helped me close countless deals...

When someone ultimately gives you that definitive no... take a breath, smile, and simply say, "May I ask you a final question?" To which they will typically respond with a "yes, sure." Then ask, "Thank you for your time, and I appreciate your responses, but I would love to know, what would it have taken from me to get a YES for this product/service/idea?"

In most cases, they stop, think, and come up with a reason. That is your moment to incorporate the reason into one final attempt to close the deal. Many times, you can turn around the sale at that moment by giving them that missing piece they wanted. It's a clever way to close and one of my go-to "Pitching Secrets."

The 3 C's: Your Closing Compass

The key to success lies in asking questions. The person asking the questions controls the conversation. So when a prospect responds to you, here's how to use the 3 C's to keep the conversation moving forward.

Imagine you're selling a coaching program. The prospect says, "I'm not sure if I'll have enough time to implement everything you teach."

- **Confirm:** The first step is to confirm what the prospect said by repeating or summarizing their question or concern. This shows active listening, builds rapport, and makes them feel heard. A dynamic way to start is to restate their concern back to them.

  > *"So you're concerned about whether you'll have enough time to implement everything inside the program. That's a great point because it shows you're serious about making sure you can fully commit."*

- **Connect:** The second step is to connect their question to the experiences of your most successful clients. For example: "That's something many of our top clients ask when making a decision. What they found, though, was that the real value came from the results they achieved..." This creates confidence and helps them see that their concerns are valid but not a dealbreaker.

  > *"A lot of my most successful clients had that exact same concern before they joined. What they found, though, was that the way we've structured our training is designed for busy people with short, actionable steps you can apply right away without feeling overwhelmed. In fact, many of them tell me it saved them time because they stopped spinning their wheels and started seeing results faster."*

- **Clarify:** The final step is to clarify by asking a follow-up question that moves the conversation forward and keeps you in control.

For example: "What's the main result you're looking for from this ____?" This clarification helps you better understand their underlying concerns and allows you to position your offer more effectively.

> *"Let me ask you, if you could carve out just 30 minutes a day, and know you were using that time to finally master your message and grow your business, would that feel doable for you?"*

Why the 3 C's Work

The 3 C's — Confirm, Connect, and Clarify—keep the conversation flowing in a way that builds a positive relationship while steering the prospect toward a decision. Each step creates a deeper connection and makes it easier to close the sale without pushing or losing credibility.

By using the 3 C's approach, you can ensure that your pitch feels natural, engaging, and ethical, which helps you turn objections into opportunities that strengthen your pitch rather than creating resistance.

Think of closing like a dance, not a wrestling match. Lead with confidence, move with purpose, and let each step flow naturally into the next. When you master this rhythm, closing becomes something you look forward to, not something you fear.

Just ask my son, Ryker—he got his candy, didn't he?

If you're excited about closing deals and mastering the 3 C's approach, head over to the Resource Center (Chapter C) and grab my favorite list of trial closes!

They make a sweet treat!

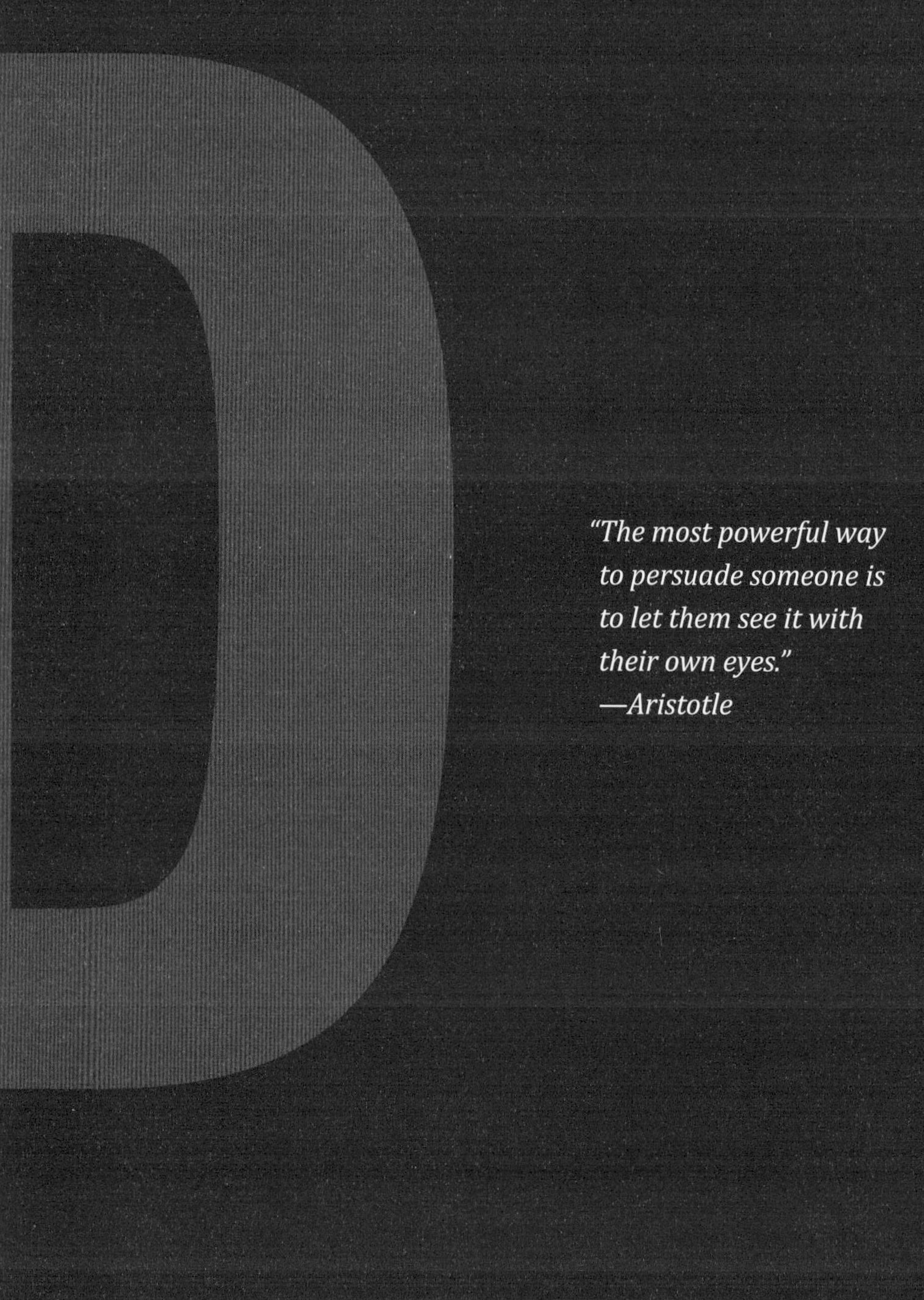

"The most powerful way to persuade someone is to let them see it with their own eyes."
—Aristotle

CHAPTER D: Demonstrate

Demonstrate (verb): *The art of showing, not just telling: using proof, visuals, and tangible results.*

We all know the saying, "talk is cheap," right? You can claim your product or service works wonders all day, but why should your prospect take your word for it? In today's world, people crave proof—something tangible that shows your offer isn't just hype; it's real. This is where the power in demonstration becomes your best friend in pitching.

To craft a winning pitch, you need more than just words. You need to *demonstrate proof.* By weaving in proof at every step, you take your pitch from mere words to concrete results. When people can *see* the impact, they trust you. They feel more confident in their decision, and guess what? They're far more likely to say "yes." So don't just tell them what your product can do—*show* them. That's how you turn skeptics into believers and leads into clients.

Why Demonstrating is So Powerful

People crave certainty, especially when it comes to spending their money or investing their time. Demonstrating what your product or service can do removes that uncertainty, validating your claims and bridging the gap between your prospect's doubts and your solution. When you provide concrete evidence, whether through before-and-after comparisons, reviews, or testimonials, it's no longer just about words. It's about undeniable proof.

This chapter explores 3 impactful strategies to incorporate proof into your pitch: showcasing transformations, leveraging customer feedback, and sharing authentic testimonials. These tools address uncertainty and build the credibility needed to inspire a resounding "yes."

Before and Afters

One of the most impactful ways to demonstrate your product's effectiveness is through before-and-after comparisons. People love a good makeover story!

And it's not just for weight loss; you can use before-and-after visuals for anything. Whether it's:

- **Home renovations** (*before:* outdated kitchen with peeling cabinets; *after:* modern, open-concept with sleek finishes)
- **Skincare results** (*before:* uneven skin tone/breakouts; *after:* clear, glowing complexion)
- **Financial transformations** (*before:* struggling with debt; *after:* achieving savings goals and financial independence)
- **Social media profiles** (*before:* low engagement; *after*: viral content)
- **Business rebranding** (*before:* an outdated logo; *after:* new cohesive identity)
- **Charity donations** (*before:* underfunded programs; *after:* thriving initiatives changing lives in the community)

This method works because it's visual. When your prospect sees the change, it's far more powerful than any description or promise. It's one thing to say, "This product helped someone lose 50 pounds," but it's another to *show* them a photo of someone who achieved that transformation. Compare the before and after and bam! The proof is right there, undeniable.

Even more exciting is when you can do this in real time. Imagine you're pitching a cleaning product. Instead of just saying it works wonders on tough stains, you take out a demo kit and show it live. You spray the product on a stubborn stain, wait a few seconds, and then wipe it away effortlessly. Or the classic demo: a knife strong enough to cut through a tin can, yet still sharp enough to glide through a ripe tomato.

Your goal is to get a "Wow!"

When you showcase a transformation effectively, your audience won't question the validity of your claims because they've witnessed the proof firsthand. Demonstrating is one of the most powerful ways to address and overcome objections.

Reviews and Ratings

We're all influenced by social proof—it's that "herd mentality" that makes us look to others for guidance. When we see others vouching for a product, we feel more confident about choosing it ourselves. In pitching, this is where reviews and ratings come in.

Think about it: How often have you scrolled through Amazon reviews before making a purchase? Those glowing reviews and high ratings push you to hit the "Buy Now" button. The same goes for pitching. When you include strong reviews from satisfied customers, it's no longer just your word—it's the word of others who have already benefited from what you're offering.

But remember, quality matters. A series of genuine result-oriented reviews will carry more weight than 100 generic ones. Your goal is to include meaningful, high-quality testimonials that paint a picture of success and reinforce trust. People want to hear real stories from others, and that social confirmation is what nudges them toward a confident "yes."

Testimonials

If there's one thing more powerful than you saying your product works, it's someone else saying it for you! Testimonials are like magic—they resolve objections, build trust, and make your pitch more relatable. Your audience witnesses real people, just like them, who have experienced the benefits of your product or service.

If a picture is worth a thousand words, then a video is worth millions . . .

While any form of testimonial is valuable to a pitch, video acts as a window to see the transformation that is possible. Unlike the written word, video is engaging, entertaining, and showcases a REAL person experiencing the benefits of your offer.

Those who have purchased and believe in your product or service are the best to speak on its behalf. Your audience sees them as a trustworthy third-party source that evokes the thought, "If it worked for them… why wouldn't it work for me?"

Here is some food for thought: Not all testimonials are the same. Some hold more power over others, such as an accredited expert in your field raving about your services.

This begs the question, what type of testimonials should you get?

Here are 3 of my favorites:

1. **Average Joe or Jane:** People connect with relatable stories. When they see someone just like them succeeding with your product, it feels authentic and achievable.
2. **Qualified Experts:** Professional endorsements bring substantial credibility. When a respected professional

backs your product, it elevates your offer in the eyes of your audience. Whether it's a quote, article, or video testimonial, expert validation shows your product holds up to industry standards.

3. **Celebrity:** A familiar face can instantly grab attention and build trust. But remember, relevance matters more than fame.

Demonstrating: The Key to Building Trust

Think of demonstrating like having a drawer full of aces—each piece of proof is a card you can play at just the right moment. But here's where most people mess up: they wait too long to show their proof. Don't make this mistake! The best pitches weave evidence throughout the entire presentation.

Your goal is to get that "wow" moment—when your audience's eyes light up and they lean in closer. Here's how:

- Show transformations happening in real time.
- Share screenshot proof of results.
- Play video testimonials at key moments.
- Use props or samples when possible.
- Tell stories that paint a vivid picture.

Start collecting *your* proof today.

Every success story, every before-and-after, every glowing review, be sure to capture them all. Because when a prospect moves from "I'm not sure" to "I want this," that shift doesn't happen by chance. It happens through a great demonstration, one that bridges the gap between uncertainty and confidence.

Remember: Don't just tell them about your magic—show them, because seeing isn't just believing... it's buying.

"Tell me and I forget, teach me and I may remember, involve me and I will learn and master it."
—Benjamin Franklin

CHAPTER E: Engage

Engage (verb): *The ability to capture attention, build connection, and create an emotional impact.*

Picture this: before I was ever known as The Queen of Pitch, I was chasing big dreams in Los Angeles, auditioning, acting, and hustling to make my mark as an actress and TV host. But what truly opened doors for me wasn't just talent; it was my ability to connect and engage with people on a deeper level.

From 1990 to 1993, I hosted the legendary Laugh Factory comedy club, sharing the stage with icons like Jerry Seinfeld, Ellen DeGeneres, and Robin Williams. I went on to become the debut host of ESPN's original X Games alongside sportscasting legend Stuart Scott. I landed my own national talk show on TLC called *Essentials*, which ran for 2 years. And I even scored every radio DJ's dream gig, hosting *Off the Record with Forbes Riley* on the world's largest radio syndication platform, Westwood One, where I got to interview music legends like Sting, Foreigner, Eric Clapton, and Journey.

But the moment that changed everything for me? It started with a pen.

I walked into what seemed like a typical commercial audition. On the desk lay a pen, a camera pointed at me, and a note that said, "Sell this pen." My first thought was how silly this was, *I am not a salesperson.* My second thought was, *How can I make myself different from all the other candidates?* I imagined most people would say the pen feels nice in their hand, it has a great roller tip, and it sells for less than a dollar. Something said if everyone is going to do that, go out on a limb and do something different.

So, I picked up the pen and rather than "sell it," I spoke from my heart:

"I went to college when I was only 16 years old. My mom used to write me longhand notes every day because of how homesick and out of place I felt. I would run to the mailbox to grab her letters in purple handwritten ink and always remember it saying at the end, 'Love Mommy.' Those letters would make me feel supported and give me the confidence to keep going with my studies no matter how hard it got."

Looking directly into the camera, I delivered the line that would change my life: "A pen like this can reach out and touch somebody's heart."

Jake "Body by Jake" Steinfeld, the man who coined the phrase "personal trainer" in the 1980s after working with Stephen Spielberg and Harrison Ford, emerged from behind the scenes and declared, "You're gonna make me a lot of money." What he saw wasn't just someone selling a pen—he saw someone who used emotion (one of the strongest buying forces) to move the listener to want to purchase. This moment led me to write and deliver on camera over 1,500 health and wellness product pitches on the cable network FitTV, which he later sold to Fox for $500 Million dollars.

Working with Jake, I crafted money-generating pitches for everything from the Suzanne Somers ThighMaster to Richard Simmons exercise DVDs, tooth whiteners and ab rollers to the latest diets and cooking gadgets. I used my relation to the product, figured out the problem they solved, the solution they offered, and added in a story that grabbed the listeners quickly. That's how I created my Ultimate Pitch Formula, which is not only the core content in one of my bestselling training programs but a tool that many people have used to make millions and get their ideas out to the world.

When presenting a product, service, or idea, you have the power to spark your audience's interest and create a desire for what you have to offer. To effectively captivate your listeners, whether it be in person, in front of a group, or on video, there is a tried-and-true process at the heart of a successful pitch.

It all boils down to how engaging you are.

Bad pitches talk numbers, data, and facts too soon. They tell people what they need without an understanding of why they really want it. And then the worst is when a pitcher hammers the features to make a sale. The inherent problem with that is, the people you are talking to are NOT YET engaged. To be effective, set the stage.

The best way to go about doing this is to pull in a heartfelt story about why you do what you do and then layer in a structured hook with a life lesson that builds emotional rapport. I call this a Springboard Story. It's a profound and effective tool that gives your pitch a human touch, making you more relatable.

Stories are a unique form of communication. It has been proven by neuroscience research that people remember and are influenced by stories much deeper than listening to facts and features.

Your Springboard Story has the capacity to give deeper context to your listener as to why they should invest their time and attention to your pitch.

More than just a simple tool, Springboard Stories must be so unique to you that no one else could tell THAT story, THAT way. They identify a universal life lesson and make an organic connection between you and your product, service, or idea.

To give you an example of this, I had a student who sold a weight loss system, with moderate sales but nowhere near the success she desired. While dissecting her pitch it came to light that she was solely focused on the product details and not her connection to the product. After working with her, we uncovered the true reason why she gained weight, lost it, and is now committed to helping others.

Her Springboard Story goes as follows:

"For 10 years I was married to a narcissistic partner who verbally and emotionally abused me. It wasn't until I mustered up the courage to leave that I realized I was an emotional overeater and when I changed my mindset, my body changed too. I regained my independence, discovered a whole new relationship to food and no longer had to rely on willpower. My system worked for me and now it's your turn!"

Then she goes into her product pitch. Her Springboard Story tripled her sales overnight because she became relatable to her audience and shared a personal insight that resonated with others.

Melissa Johnson

I used to think success was all about credentials, the perfect pitch, and a polished presentation... until I discovered the power of the Springboard Story with Forbes Riley. 🤯

In just minutes, she showed me how to take my personal struggles and turn them into a story that made people lean in, connect, and say YES! 🙌

If you're struggling to make an impact, trust me—your story is the key. And no one teaches this better than Forbes!

Another great example is a student I had who designed artistic cultural coloring books, but was blocked on how to pitch them.

She couldn't figure out how to connect a Springboard Story to her product. So we dug deep into the past. After much thought, she revealed her childhood. Growing up during the Cold War in East Germany, a bleak, gray world filled with landmines, guard dogs, and a lack of hope. Enduring this emotional imprisonment, she dreamed of beautiful places to visit and found herself coloring with the few markers she had found to help her escape the madness around her.

Many years later she became an international flight attendant and created a cultural coloring book to excite young people about the beauty in the world beyond their current situation.

Can you feel the difference? This story took a simple coloring book that struggled to sell on Amazon to a global sensation.

The Springboard Story has the power to transform any pitch into a captivating, high-impact experience.

When told right, your story doesn't just explain—it moves people. It makes your pitch unforgettable.

Because when an audience is truly engaged, they don't just hear you—**they believe you, remember you, and act because of you.**

If you're ready to explore how your personal journey can elevate your business, product, and influence, head to Chapter E in the *Pitch Secrets A to Z*, free Resource Center.

Scan the QR Code to unlock access.

"Build the illusion to achieve the dream."
—Forbes Riley

CHAPTER F: Forbes It

"Forbes It" (verb): *To manifest something, especially when it seems impossible or improbable to do.*

The name FORBES in my family symbolizes 3 generations of independence, innovative ideas, and defying the impossible.

My story begins with my grandparents immigrating from Ukraine to the US to escape persecution in their homeland, only to discover the same antisemitism existed here in the United States. My grandmother Tillie, a fierce Jewish mother in mid-20th century America, watched her brilliant sons be denied college entry simply because their last name, Feinstein, revealed their heritage. In a bold move that would change our family's destiny, she opened a phone book and chose a random last name, "Forbes." That single act of courage gave my father and uncle the chance to pursue their dreams of becoming engineers.

They succeeded not because they changed who they were, but because they changed how the world saw them. This is the essence of "Forbesing It"—making bold, creative moves to create opportunities where none seem to exist.

Growing up on Long Island in a lower-middle-class family, I watched my dad tinker with inventions and perform magic tricks while my mom collected celebrity autographs of people she dreamed of meeting. Their life was modest but fulfilling. Yet I heard them say too often, "Success isn't for people like us."

Those words shaped how I initially viewed my potential and would ring in my head as I looked in the mirror at an overweight, frizzy haired young girl with a mouth full of metal braces and a badly crooked nose. I was the farthest thing from the glamorous Hollywood actresses

I idolized in the movies. Then to make matters worse, while I was in high school, my dad slipped at work and caught his hand in a printing press. He would then spend the next 3 years in the hospital and after 15 surgeries to reconstruct his hand, my family was financially devastated. I remember my mom saying, "That's just our life, good things don't happen to people like us." That's when it hit me: I was not going to sit down and accept fate. I was going to take my life into my own hands.

With the help of my dad's doctor, who generously offered to fix my nose for free, and my mom's suggestion that the Miss Teenage America pageant was offering a college scholarship, I found myself at a crossroads. This was the first time I decided to truly *Forbes* something—no one believed the awkward, shy, "ugly duckling" could win a beauty pageant.

Fueled by a fierce determination to outgrow my family's struggles and prove the impossible, I pulled together a hand-me-down bridesmaid dress, my old tap shoes, and an unwavering sense of purpose. For the first time, I felt the fire to create my own path—not just to save my family financially, but to follow my dreams and shape my future.

Defying all odds, I won Miss Teenage New York, received a college scholarship, and the opportunity to stand next to Bob Hope on NBC to compete in the Nationals.

This was the first time I ever felt like I could do anything, so I ran with it. I used the scholarship to go to college, graduating in 3 years with 2 degrees (majoring in Political Science with a minor in History, and Communications with a minor in Performing Arts), and then headed off to pursue my acting dreams in New York City. Initially, things went well: I landed the lead in my first feature film audition (albeit, a low-budget horror film called *Splatter University*), ended up on Broadway with the original "Superman," Christopher Reeve, and landed small parts in various soap operas. I was becoming the vision I had always dreamed of, but after a while, I had hit the ceiling of my career in New York.

That's when I took the leap to move out to California, hoping for a fresh start. Except... Hollywood wasn't as welcoming as I had hoped. Audition after audition, rejection after rejection, I wasn't the right "type." Not pretty enough. Not famous enough. Not thin enough. Not *enough*.

I hit the lowest financial point of my adult life. My partner at the time could see my frustration of not fitting the mold of what casting directors were looking for so he suggested I visit an image consultant. It sounded ridiculous; wasn't I already doing everything I could? But I was out of options, so I went...

That consultant, in just one hour, changed my life. He asked me, "*What do you see when you look in the mirror?*"

I mumbled something about being an actress, a TV host, a struggling artist. Then he said something that *shook* me.

"You're not stepping into the power of who you need to be. To become what you want, you need to shift how you believe in yourself."

That's when it clicked. I had been waiting for success to find me when I needed to become the *kind* of person success *wants* to find. I looked at the greats: actors, artists, icons. Many of them had reinvented themselves:

- Jennifer Linn Anastassakis → **Jennifer Aniston**
- Norma Jean Baker → **Marilyn Monroe**
- Mark Sinclair → **Vin Diesel**
- Eric Bishop → **Jamie Foxx**
- Christopher Brian Bridges → **Ludacris**
- Peter Gene Hernandez → **Bruno Mars**
- Stefani Joanne Angelina Germanotta → **Lady Gaga**

So, like my grandmother before me, I made a bold decision. Francine Forbes, the shy, scared little girl, became Forbes Riley—a woman bold enough to chase her dreams.

At first, it felt like an act. After all, I was an actress; creating characters was second nature. But over time, Forbes Riley became my truth: powerful, fearless, and unstoppable. And while I didn't end up starring in big-budget Hollywood films the way I once dreamed, I carved out a career that was anything but ordinary. For 3 incredible years, I found a home on stage as the host of the legendary Laugh Factory, Los Angeles's premiere comedy club, where I shared the mic with icons like Robin Williams, Jerry Seinfeld, Ellen DeGeneres, Jamie Foxx, and Chris Rock.

Beyond the comedy world, I helped launch several pioneering cable networks, including FitTV, TLC, and Animal Planet. I also had the honor of co-hosting the original ESPN X-Games alongside broadcasting legend Stuart Scott, bringing extreme sports into the mainstream for the very first time.

And in a world where few women had a seat at the table, I became a trailblazer in the billion-dollar infomercial industry—writing, producing, and pitching products that would go on to change lives and break sales records.

The path of my career has not been something I imagined, but it has surpassed my wildest dreams, and my only regret is that both my parents passed away before they could see what happens when you let go of limiting beliefs.

Fear had held me back for so long, but I realized something:

Fear isn't your enemy!

That nervous energy before a big pitch? It's not telling you to stop; it's telling you this moment matters. Fear is your body's way of saying, "Pay attention. This is important." When you reframe fear this way, it becomes a motivator instead of anxiety.

To "Forbes It" means to take what scares you and use it as rocket fuel for your dreams. It means seeing obstacles as opportunities and the word "impossible" as an invitation. When someone says it can't be done, that's your cue to prove them wrong.

Here's How YOU Forbes It:

1. **Identify what you fear.** Your biggest fears often point directly to your most important goals.
2. **Define your dream.** Not what others expect, but what *you* truly want. Write it down. Make it real.
3. **Commit fully.** No more hesitation. No more waiting for the *perfect* moment. Decide.
4. **Take bold action.** Even small steps, taken consistently, create unstoppable momentum.
5. **Build your success squad.** Surround yourself with people who *believe* in your vision.
6. **Celebrate every victory.** Each small win builds the confidence for bigger ones.
7. **Own your power.** You're not just *capable* of achieving your dreams—you're *worthy* of them.

When you *Forbes It*, something incredible happens: you start achieving things others call *impossible*.

I know because I've lived it. I've *Forbes'd* my way onto stages, into TV shows, into business success, and into a life beyond my wildest childhood dreams.

My greatest joy has been watching my students and clients *Forbes-ing* their own dreams into reality:

"I Forbes'd launching my own podcast and running marathons after losing my sight as a child and being told I would never live a full, independent life."

"I Forbes'd my way from war-torn Russia, where I stood in bread lines wearing a gray uniform, to becoming a celebrated American fashion designer dressing the world in color."

"I Forbes'd my way onto the biggest stages as a sought-after public speaker—after growing up in an abusive household where I was told to be quiet and that my voice didn't matter."

"I Forbes'd my way out of the cycle of poverty, rewriting my story from barely making ends meet to running a thriving seven-figure construction company."

"I Forbes'd losing over 100 lbs—not just for my health, but because I finally decided that I mattered, and now I coach others to achieve their fitness goals."

When you *Forbes It*, you're not just changing your own life—you're showing others what's possible. Think about Roger Bannister in 1954. For years, experts declared running a mile in under 4 minutes was physically impossible. The human body simply couldn't do it, they said. But Bannister didn't just break the record—he shattered a universal belief. Within 46 days, another runner did the same. Today, over 1,600 athletes have accomplished what was once "impossible." That's the power of one person daring to *Forbes It*—they break through the wall of "impossible" so others can follow.

Now, it's *your* turn.

This is your moment to step into your power, to turn "I can't" into "I will," to *Forbes It*. The world is waiting for your impossible dream to become reality.

So I ask you: What will YOU *Forbes* in your life *right now*?

____

____

____

Remember: When they say it can't be done, *that's exactly when you Forbes It.*

Are you ready to make it happen?

Take a picture of what your *Forbes'd It* goal is and share it in our community Facebook group. Let's support each other in making the impossible, possible.

Scan the QR Code to post.

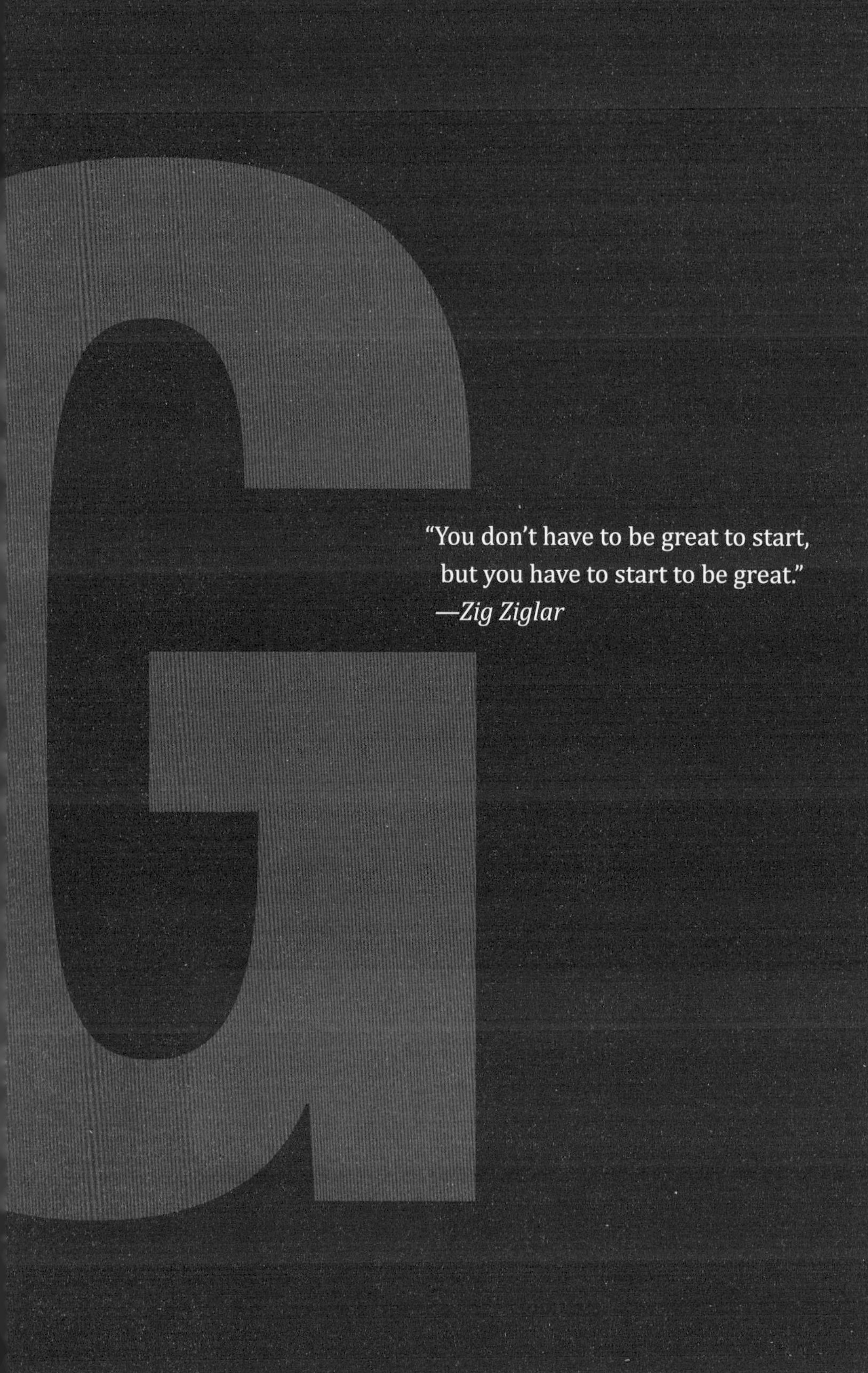

"You don't have to be great to start,
but you have to start to be great."
—*Zig Ziglar*

CHAPTER G: Goals

Goals (noun): *The bridge between dreams and measurable success, turning ambition into actionable steps that drive real results.*

Here's a truth that might sting: The difference between dreamers and achievers isn't talent or luck—it's the audacity to set outrageous goals, and the guts to chase them down. Let me show you what I mean.

I was at an event when I had the privilege of hearing Les Brown deliver one of his unforgettable motivational speeches about finding your personal greatness. For years, I was an actress, bringing characters to life and delivering lines that someone else had written. I loved the craft, the connection, and the energy of performing, but something always felt… incomplete. I wasn't saying my words. I wasn't telling *my* story. And as much as I adored acting, I realized it wasn't enough to fulfill the deep desire I had to make a lasting impact.

That realization sparked a new outrageous goal: I wanted to become a motivational speaker and share the lessons I'd learned, the obstacles I'd overcome, and the truths that had transformed my own life, inspiring millions of people to chase their dreams.

The next question, of course, was: *How do I achieve this?* So many people get stuck at this point, trapped in the uncertainty of "*How am I going to make this happen?*"

Something inside me said, "*Go big or go home.*" If I was going to make this happen, I had to aim for the stars. So, I started searching for the biggest conferences where I could potentially speak. That's when I discovered the 10X Growth Conference by Grant Cardone in 2018. At the time, Grant wasn't the household name he is today, but he was already hosting an event with a massive audience of 10,000 people. As I scanned the lineup of speakers, I noticed something: it was dominated by men. That's when it hit me: this was my chance to break barriers, represent women on that stage, and leave a lasting impression.

I'd heard Grant was going to be in Las Vegas attending a real estate conference, so I thought, *no problem... I'll go, get a ticket, and we can have lunch.* The universe has a unique sense of humor; no matter what I did I could not get into this event. There were no tickets available, no guest spots, no special contacts... I was on the brink of giving up until it happened. That night I was walking down one of the long casino hallways and at the other end walking toward me was Grant, his wife, and his entourage. This was my 60-second window to make it happen.

The old me would have babbled, listed off my accomplishments to try to impress him, and I'd have completely blown the opportunity. But I didn't. I had a powerful goal clearly in my head and the action step was simply getting him to agree to meet properly. This is the epitome of the elevator pitch I teach.

As I approached, I remember thinking, his wife Elena probably wouldn't appreciate some random woman walking up to her husband. So I turned to her and said, "It's nice to meet you, Elena. I'm a successful infomercial host who's grossed over $2.5 Billion dollars in product sales. I think that your husband could elevate his career even higher by being in an infomercial."

Without hesitation, she turned to Grant and said, "You need to meet this woman," which I interpreted as the perfect introduction. I looked at him, did my elevator pitch, and *boom*... he invited me to a dinner party they were hosting to talk more.

At one point during the night, I had my opportunity to speak with Grant, and the next thing I knew, we were talking about there not being enough women on his upcoming 10X stage. He recognized the need and was so impressed, he booked me to speak.

That, my friend, is how creating a specific goal, knowing how to pitch, and being bold enough to step outside of your comfort zone will create your dreams.

I remember stepping onto that stage, fully present, knowing everything had led to this. What unfolded became a speech that left an undeniable imprint—one still spoken about today. It didn't happen by chance. It was born from a goal set long before the lights, the crowd, or the applause. You can watch that speech in the Resource Center under Chapter G.

Goals help you concentrate your energy and give direction to your actions. They can bring out the best in you and help to eliminate negative tendencies, such as procrastination or babbling.

When it comes to pitching, clarity is key. If you want to be effective and use your time wisely, you need to set defined, actionable goals. Otherwise, you're not really pitching; you're just talking. And in my experience, that means you're wasting both breath and opportunity.

To help you maximize your time and make sure you accomplish all the necessary steps to achieve your pitching goals, I've created a 5-step goal acronym, P.I.T.C.H:

P is for Purpose: Your first goal is to be 100% clear on what you're pitching and why you're pitching it. I find many people tend to just start speaking and go off on unrelated tangents completely confusing their prospect and causing them to lose interest.

I is for Identify: Your second goal is to recognize who you're pitching and why they would be interested in what you're offering. The innovative way to do this is to ask questions and make strategic assumptions about your prospect.

T is for Technique: Your third goal is to understand how you are showing up. A great pitch isn't just about what you say—it's how you say it. From your tone of voice to your body language, every element should exude confidence and authenticity. Mastering your technique can make the difference between a lukewarm response and an enthusiastic "Yes!"

C is for Connection: Your fourth goal is to build a genuine rapport. People don't buy from pitches; they buy from people they trust and resonate with. Use storytelling, humor, or shared experiences to create a bond that goes beyond the product or service you're offering. A strong connection transforms a prospect into a trusted ally.

H is for Hustle: Your fifth goal is to bring relentless action to your pitch. Success doesn't happen by chance—it requires consistent effort, follow-up, and persistence. Hustle means showing up prepared, going the extra mile, and staying committed even when the initial response isn't a resounding yes. When you combine passion with determination, you create opportunities that others might miss.

Here's what most goal-setting advice gets wrong: They tell you to be "realistic." But realistic goals don't inspire realistic action. They inspire realistic excuses. When you set a goal that scares you, that's when you find out what you're really capable of.

Standing on that 10X stage, looking out at 10,000 faces, I realized something profound. Goals aren't just about what you achieve—they're about who you become in the process. Every "impossible" goal you chase transforms you. Each barrier you break makes you bigger.

Remember: *Goals without deadlines are just wishes. Dreams without action are just sleep. And pitches without purpose are just conversation.*

You might be wondering right now, *How did Forbes Riley strategically set her goals to become a $2.5 Billion-dollar host, a world-renowned speaker, and build the most loving and wonderful family?*

Here's my secret: I have a goal journal. Sure, you can type things out, but there's something magical about physically writing down your goals—it creates a powerful connection to your vision. Since my 20s, I've written down every dream, every idea, every goal I've wanted to achieve. And here's the amazing part: they came true!

A Goal Journal isn't just another notebook; it's your personal roadmap to success. It's where dreams transform into deadlines, where "someday" becomes "today," and where your big break gets planned before it happens. Whether you choose your own journal or grab my specially designed Goal Setting Journey from the Resource Center, this is your tool for turning impossible into inevitable.

Once you have committed to a particular outcome, do whatever it takes to achieve that aim regardless of the effort it requires, the time it takes, or the difficulties that arise along the way.

It's time for you to start Forbesing your life.

Achieving goals is a level of happiness that very few things equate to.

Want to start setting and achieving goals that matter?

Scan the QR Code to grab your Goal Journal from the Resource Center (Chapter G).

But fair warning—once you start achieving the impossible... it becomes addictive.

"The most powerful pitch you'll ever make doesn't start with your words — it starts with your handshake."
—Forbes Riley

CHAPTER H: Handshake

Handshake (noun): *A physical gesture symbolic of establishing connections and building trust.*

It is believed that the act of shaking hands originated in prehistoric times as a means of demonstrating peaceful intentions. With the passing of time, the handshake evolved into a formal way for two2 individuals to greet one another.

Something I've noticed from years of networking is that most people have never been taught how to do a proper handshake. Let's recap before diving into how to make it a moment that matters. When you initially meet someone, here are the steps to follow:

1. **Start with a smile** to create a sense of invitation.
2. **Hold eye contact** and stay present in the moment.
3. **Extend your right hand** and grasp theirs.
4. **Keep it firm**—not overpowering, but confident.
5. **Maintain** eye contact throughout the interaction.

A strong handshake isn't just a greeting; it's the foundation of someone's first impression of you and an instant way to build rapport. But here's the real opportunity: how do you turn a handshake into an engaging connection?

It starts by understanding that a handshake and your pitch are no longer isolated; they are seamlessly integrated.

In the first 60 seconds of a handshake you have the listener's undivided attention... So why not capitalize on it? A handshake or any other form of introduction can serve as the initial pitch to who you are and what you do. It's your first chance to make an unforgettable impression.

Picture this: you're at a networking event, you shake someone's hand, and then they ask you the inevitable question, "So, what do you do?"

Most people rush through their introduction like they're ticking off a laundry list. Big mistake! The truth is, the person asking doesn't care about all the things you do. What they really want to know is: *What can you do for them?*

Let me share something that completely changed my pitching game. Years ago, when people would ask what I do, I'd launch into this long-winded response about being an actress, infomercial host, fitness expert, and speaker... and I'd watch their eyes glaze over faster than a donut at Krispy Kreme!

Even worse, when I'd simply say, "I'm a movie and film actress and I host TV shows," they'd immediately jump to "Wow, what have you been in?" or "Do you know any celebrities?"

Then it hit me: Nobody wants to hear my résumé. They want to know how I could solve their problems and their pain points. That's what matters. Once I stopped leading with my résumé and started focusing on *how I could make someone's life better*, everything changed. Conversations opened up. Opportunities appeared. Networking stopped feeling transactional and became transformational.

That shift began with one moment: **The Handshake**. I stopped answering, *"What do you do?"* with a laundry list of titles. Instead, I crafted a response that made people lean in and say, *"Tell me more."*

Now, when someone asks what I do, I say:

> "I'm known as the Queen of Pitch. After selling billions on TV, I now teach entrepreneurs how to communicate with confidence so they can close more deals without ever sounding salesy."

See the difference? That simple change from a title to a transformation can be the difference between sparking a powerful connection… or watching it walk away.

So it's time to rethink the Handshake.

Don't just give a technical answer. Give a compelling one. Don't just share what you *do*. Share what you *make possible*. Because the right words in the first 30 seconds can open the door to your next big opportunity.

Here is an example: which one inspires you to take action and continue the conversation further?

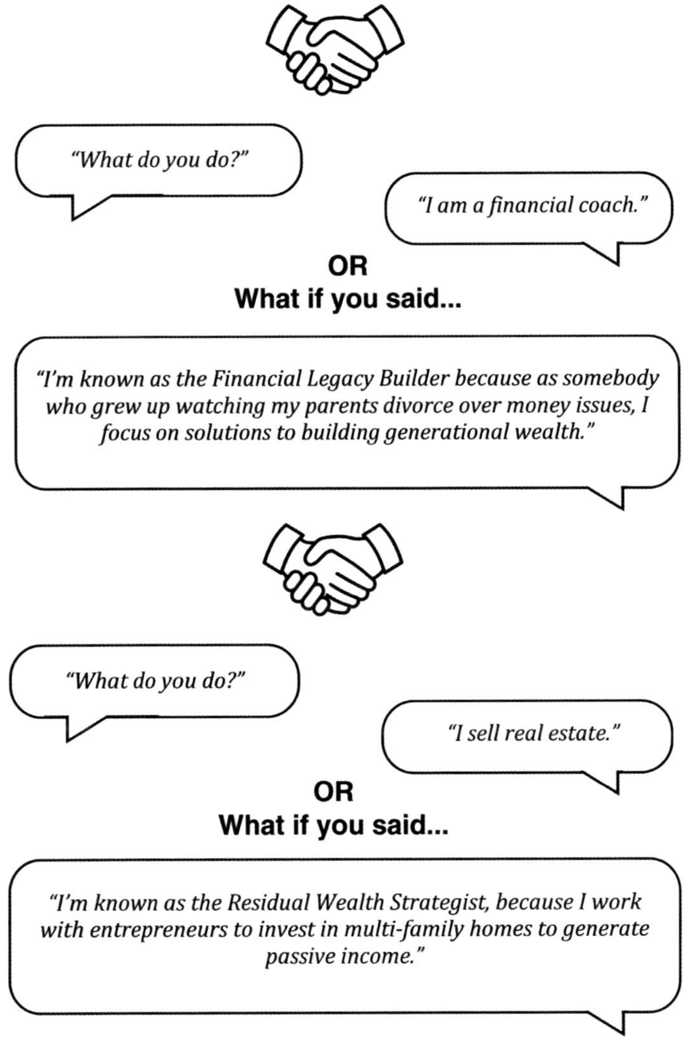

Most people are not consciously aware of this, but in those first moments of asking "What do you do?" your new acquaintance is deciding whether or not you're a useful connection to them and if they should continue the conversation.

One tells them what you do, the other tells them what you can do for THEM.

Here is my Handshake Strategy to make the most out of every networking event.

THE 3 PHASES OF THE HANDSHAKE

Phase 1: The Pre-Handshake

Always think one step ahead.

Before attending any event, have a clear goal in mind. Answer these key questions to set yourself up for success:

- **What type of event is it?**
- **Why are you there?**
- **What is your goal?**
- **What can I do for the people in attendance?**

Phase 2: The Handshake

Once you answer the pre-handshake questions, it's time to put together your "What do you do?" response. This is only 1–2 sentences that tell someone who you are, why you do what you do, and what you can do for them.

No one wants to hear your entire life story, but if you can give them context and credibility to what you do within that response, you hit the gold mine.

This leads to your prospect having an open mind about your product or service and being enthusiastic about hearing more. The perfect segue to your elevator pitch.

The goal isn't to sell them immediately but to capture interest, enroll them in your vision, and leave your listener wanting more—giving you the room to nurture the connection into something bigger.

Phase 3: Post-Handshake

If you do the first two stages right, there will undoubtedly be another opportunity for you to engage with your prospect and have them purchase what you offer. This is your time to follow up and solidify this new contact.

Statistics show that 60% of deals happen during follow-up. That means your handshake is just the beginning. Within 48 hours of meeting someone new:

- Send a personalized email or text.
- Connect on relevant social platforms.
- Share a specific resource that adds value.
- Or better yet, send a handwritten note (you'd be amazed how this small touch makes you unforgettable; emails can be overlooked, snail mail is impossible to ignore).

In conclusion, your next handshake could be your million-dollar moment. The question is: Will you treat it like a forgettable formality, or will you use it to open doors you never thought possible?

When introducing yourself it's crucial to go beyond generic labels. While titles like engineer, digital marketer, doctor, or business owner are correct, they lack the depth, context, and connection needed to truly captivate. Instead, leverage your backstory and/or credibility to build an element that leads them to say, "Tell Me More."

A handshake is more than a gesture—it's a promise, a moment of connection that says, *"I see you. I respect you. Let's build something together."* In a world that moves fast and often forgets the human touch, a single handshake can be the start of trust, transformation, and opportunity.

So the next time you reach out your hand, do it with presence. Do it with purpose. Because when energy meets intention, what starts as a handshake... can turn into a life-changing deal.

I've created a proven blueprint for maximizing your introductory handshake, so it leaves a lasting impact, sparks curiosity, and opens doors.

It's not about rehearsed lines or stiff formality. It's about showing up with clarity, confidence, and charisma that makes people lean in and want to know more.

Scan the QR Code if you're ready to uplevel and turn your initial meeting into a game-changer.

"Life's a pitch and then you buy."
—Billy Mays

CHAPTER I: Infomercial

Infomercial (noun): *A long-form advertisement that blends entertainment and education to demonstrate, persuade, and drive immediate action.*

"But wait, there's more!"

A simple phrase that changed the face of marketing—transforming quick 30-*second* commercials into 30-*minute* infomercials. Let me take you back to where it all began.

In the late 1980s, there were only 5 major TV stations running soap operas, morning talk shows, and news programs during the day—but when night fell, television went dark. Then came cable TV, bursting onto the scene with more than 500 channels running 24/7. Networks suddenly had endless airtime but no profitable way to fill those late-night hours.

The solution? A 30-minute "show" that turned dead airtime into prime real estate: the infomercial. This transformed what had been a financial drain into a gold mine of opportunity. Infomercials flipped the script—literally—by introducing a bold, innovative pitching style that entertained while it sold. It was marketing with a heartbeat, a show with purpose, and it forever changed how products were presented to the world.

This new format didn't just open doors for advertisers; it opened a brand-new world for *me*. At the time, I was working in Los Angeles as an actress, caught between 2 eras of marketing: the traditional and the emerging. I'd audition for 60-second commercials and, to be 100% transparent... I wasn't great at them. Casting directors would hand me lines like, "It's not just for breakfast anymore," or "I'm lovin' it!"—then expect me to flash a perfect smile at the camera. I rarely got booked.

Then one day, everything changed. I walked into what I thought was another typical audition—just another chance to smile, deliver a one-liner, and hope for the best. But this time, the casting assistant handed me a script that was 5 pages long! It wasn't a jingle; it was a story. There was dialogue, humor, energy—actual conversation. I remember thinking, *this feels more like a TV show than a commercial*. The script called for chemistry, for playfulness, for real connection between 2 people. That's when something clicked. I spotted a guy in the lobby who looked like he could've been the fifth Beatle and said, "Hey, want to rehearse this with me?" His name was Robin Letvinchuk, a news anchor from Canada. We hit it off instantly, nailed the audition, and both booked the job.

That shoot changed everything. It was one of the very first infomercials ever to air on television—promoting a product called QMI, an automotive oil additive. Between Robin's and my natural chemistry and our on-camera interview with racing legend Bobby Unser, the show became a massive hit. I earned more from that single shoot than I'd ever made in my entire acting career.

That moment marked the birth of something extraordinary. What began as a onetime gig turned into a full-blown revolution and my new calling. This wave of bold, long-form advertising propelled me into hosting hundreds of infomercials, earning recognition as one of the most successful female presenters in the world. Over the years, I would take home awards for *Best Host, Best Product,* and *Best Infomercial* again and again.

I was part of a pioneering movement that completely redefined television advertising—an industry that would go on to generate over **$250 Billion** in product sales by 2015. The traditional 30-second commercial couldn't compete with what we had created: storytelling that sold.

After that first big win, I was hooked. Suddenly, I wasn't just acting; I was communicating in a way that made people *feel something*. Every infomercial became its own mini-movie, a stage where I could combine storytelling, education, and emotion to move people into action. I wasn't just reading lines anymore; I was creating transformation on camera.

In those early days, we were inventing the rules as we went. We experimented with tone, pacing, and demonstrations—anything that could capture attention and keep viewers from changing the channel. We learned quickly that the secret wasn't in the script; it was in the *connection*. When people saw real results, real emotion, and real passion, they didn't just buy the product; they bought into the possibility of a better life.

I started to study what worked and what didn't. Why did one show make millions while another fizzled? Why did some presenters instantly connect while others fell flat? The answer was always the same: the pitch. The ability to excite, engage, and enroll an audience into a vision. Every great infomercial followed a rhythm, a sequence that guided viewers from curiosity to conviction to action.

Those late nights on set taught me lessons no business school ever could. I learned how to speak to human desire, not just the product features. I learned how to transform skepticism into trust, and hesitation into action. That's when I realized this wasn't just television—it was *psychology in motion*.

That moment became the foundation of every powerful pitch I would teach for the rest of my career. When you boil it down, every blockbuster infomercial shares one secret ingredient: **the pitch**. It wasn't just what we said; it was how we said it. The rhythm, the energy, the story that turned late-night viewers into believers.

Infomercials worked because they followed a proven structure—one that excites, engages, and enrolls. Whether someone was in a studio, a living room, or lying in bed in their pajamas, the psychology never changed. When emotion meets clarity, action follows.

A great pitch is the blueprint behind every sale and every "yes." Once you master it, you can use it anywhere—on stage, in a webinar, or online.

So let's pull back the curtain. Here's **The 9-Step Video Pitch**—the timeless framework that's generated billions in sales and still drives the most persuasive marketing today.

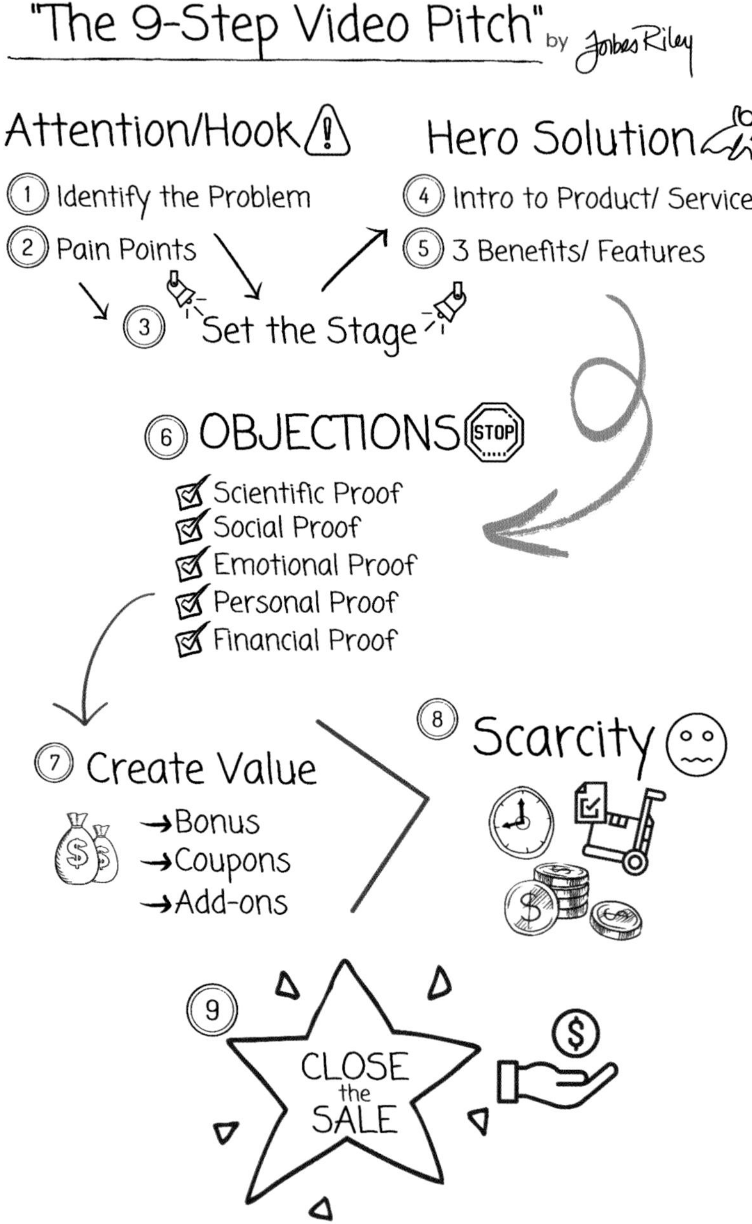

1. **Grab Attention:** Open with an irresistible hook that instantly captivates your audience by highlighting the core problem they're facing.
2. **Identify Pain Points:** Uncover the specific struggles your audience is facing so you can position your solution as the answer they've been searching for.
3. **Set the Stage:** Paint the scene by walking your audience through a relatable story, asking a compelling question, or sharing statistics that dive deeper into the challenges they're experiencing.
4. **Introduce Hero Solution:** Transition into your product or service as the ultimate answer to their problem using 3 key features and benefits. For maximum impact include before and afters or persuasive demos to showcase results.
5. **Pinpoint Features and Benefits:** Highlight what your product or service does (features) and, more importantly, how it improves your audience's life (benefits).
6. **Overcome Objections:** Proactively address doubts using data, testimonials, endorsements, or value comparisons to eliminate resistance before it even surfaces.
7. **Create Value:** Enhance your offer with bonuses, coupons, or add-ons that make your audience feel the urgency and exclusivity of saying yes right now.
8. **Determine Scarcity:** Build urgency by emphasizing a limited-time offer, low inventory, or an upcoming price increase to inspire immediate action.
9. **Close the Sale:** Deliver a powerful, clear call to action that combines urgency with simple next steps, making it easy for your audience to say yes now.

This formula led me to write, produce, and host 197 infomercials, generating billions in sales. Over my career I worked with Jack LaLanne promoting the Power Juicer (selling $1 Billion worth of product across 80 countries) to launching one of Kim Kardashian's first appearances on television with the Pressa Bella steam iron (a year before her reality TV show), and working alongside legends such as Billy Mays, George Foreman, Billy Blanks, Florence Henderson, Mario Lopez, Tony Little, Montel Williams, and more.

I had the privilege of creating and perfecting the pitches behind simple products that became global sensations, earning the iconic label *"As Seen on TV."*

Then in the mid-2000s everything changed. Streaming and the internet began replacing the traditional watching experience and audiences' attention plus buying power was moving online quickly.

While the medium was shifting, the basic nature and structure of the video pitch always stayed the same.

Pioneering digital marketers became enamored with the pitching structure of the infomercial and it inspired early concepts that swept the internet, like the Visual Sales Letters and webinars. Once again, the power of this structured pitch began making outrageous sales and printing money.

Want to see these timeless principles in action? Check out some of my most successful infomercials under Chapter I in the Resource Center, including the billion-dollar Power Juicer phenomenon and Kim Kardashian's first TV appearance in our steam iron show. You'll start to see the patterns and psychology that turn viewers into buyers, skeptics into believers, and ordinary pitches into extraordinary opportunities.

Look at today's digital landscape. The same principles that made infomercials generate billions are driving today's most successful social media campaigns and influencer content. Whether it's a viral TikTok or a Facebook ad, the psychology remains timeless: connect authentically, demonstrate value, and make people feel part of something special.

The platforms may have changed, but human nature remains the same. From the iconic "Call Right Now" to today's "Like and Subscribe," people are still driven to take action when the pitch is right. The methods may look different, but the core of what captivates and converts remains unchanged.

Let me take you behind the scenes and introduce you to some of the biggest names in the infomercial industry who not only inspired me, but changed the way we promote and pitch products around the globe!

Andy Latimer and Brian Fasulo—Working with the Bluewater Media Team was an extraordinary experience. Andy's vision and leadership built one of the most innovative production and marketing powerhouses in the industry, while Brian's creative genius and results-driven storytelling turned every campaign into a record-breaking success. Together, they brought projects to life with unmatched expertise delivering campaigns built to outlast trends and outshine the competition. One of my longest friendships in the infomercial industry excited for our future!

Beau Rials—Working with Beau was a masterclass in connection and conversion. With over 200 infomercials and more than $2 billion in sales under his belt, he brings an unmatched presence to every set. Every time we co-hosted, I watched him effortlessly build trust with the audience in seconds. He's got that rare blend of charm, expertise, and precision that makes you lean in and say, "I want that." Collaborating with Beau wasn't just fun—it was next-level. He made the products shine, made me a better host, and together, we created television that truly moved people to action.

Billy Blanks—I had the honor of working with Billy Blanks before Tae Bo became a global phenomenon. As host of *Essentials*, I gave him his first national TV spotlight—and the world took notice. His passion was undeniable, and our collaboration proved how the right pitch at the right time can ignite a movement. Together, we championed strength from the inside out.

Bill Guthy and Greg Renker—Working with Guthy-Renker founders Bill and Greg was inspiring. Visionaries in direct-to-consumer marketing, they launched industry-changing brands like Proactiv, Meaningful Beauty, and The Principal Secret. Their ability to craft groundbreaking pitches and build global brands set new standards, turning dreams into household names.

Bruce (now Caitlyn) Jenner—Here with the Olympic Gold Medalist, filming our vitamin/ wellness infomercial. The dedication to excellence showed in everything—from athletics to pitching products. This collaboration led to an interesting twist in my pitching journey: I was then introduced to Kris Jenner, which resulted in me casting Kim Kardashian in a steam iron infomercial, just before *Keeping Up with the Kardashians* catapulted the family to superstardom. A perfect example of how authentic relationships can open unexpected doors!

Carl Daikeler—Working with Carl on the Power90 infomercial was akin to witnessing a vision come to life. Long before *Beachbody* became a household name, Carl had a mission: to transform lives through fitness, mindset, and community. I saw firsthand the passion, innovation, and relentless drive that built a billion-dollar brand. To this day, I'm proud to have been part of the early chapter of that incredible journey.

Chef Richard Blais and Chef Robert Irvine—Talk about a recipe for success! Working with Chef champion Richard Blais and Chef Robert Irvine proved how passion spices up any pitch. Richard brought molecular gastronomy to kitchens on *Top Chef University*. Robert, before *Restaurant: Impossible*, co-hosted a non-stick cookware infomercial that launched his TV career. Two chefs, one key ingredient: infectious enthusiasm that keeps audiences hungry for more!

Cory Everson—I had the thrill of co-hosting 3 fitness shows with the legendary 6x Ms. Olympia, Cory Everson. Her fierce dedication to fitness and vast expertise set a high bar, and our combined energy brought intensity and impact to each show. Cory's generosity and authentic positivity brought out the best in everyone around her. Together, we inspired viewers to chase their strongest selves, proving that real empowerment isn't just about personal strength—it's about lifting each other up.

Dr. Bill Dorfman—I first met Bill at HSN, where he was transforming smiles and I was transforming pitches. He's not only the reason I have the best smile on camera, but also one of the most brilliant teachers and pitchmen I know. From dentistry to the LEAP Foundation, Bill empowers people to lead, speak, and shine—and I'm grateful to call him a mentor and friend.

Dr. Drew Ordon—Hosting Dr. Drew's infomercial and joining him on his TV series The Doctors (with SpinGym) was an incredible blend of our worlds. With his medical expertise and my passion for pitching, we turned complex health solutions into something anyone could understand and take action on. Bringing SpinGym to that stage reminded me how powerful the right partnership and the right pitch can be in changing lives.

Ed Crain—Working with Ed was like collaborating with a master strategist. Behind the scenes of some of our most successful infomercials, including our unforgettable work with Jack LaLanne, Ed brought the perfect balance of creative vision and business precision. His deep understanding of the global DRTV markets allowed us to turn big ideas into even bigger sales. I've always said pitching is part art, part science and Ed is one of the rare few who mastered both and often brought me along for the ride!

Florence Henderson—Teaming up with America's favorite mom from *The Brady Bunch*, we brought timeless beauty to the screen with our unforgettable skincare show. Who better to showcase ageless skincare than an icon who defined grace and charm for generations? With Florence's warmth and my passion for pitching, we showed that beauty truly knows no bounds or age limits! Together, we proved that glowing skin is always in style, no matter what decade you're in.

George Foreman—Best known, not only for his boxing career but for revolutionizing kitchens worldwide with the George Foreman Grill. His pitch wasn't just about selling a product; it was about a healthier, simpler lifestyle that resonated with millions. Watching him bring that passion to life and seeing the impact of his pitch skills in creating a household name was truly inspiring. George proved that the right pitch can turn an idea into a global phenomenon!

Jay Cutler—Filming a vitamin infomercial with Jay Cutler, a 4x Mr. Olympia and a true icon in bodybuilding, revealed just how much dedication and resilience translate into the art of the pitch. Jay's approach was rooted in discipline, focus, and a lifetime commitment to excellence. He reminded me that an impactful pitch is much like his training: it demands precision, consistency, and authenticity. Together, we conveyed a message of wellness with the same strength and sincerity he brings to everything he does.

Joe Theismann—He is the legendary NFL quarterback and former Super Bowl champion, known for leading the Redskins football team and later as a successful sports broadcaster. I had the opportunity to work with Joe on an award-winning infomercial for Barefoot Science insoles. His ability to communicate clearly and passionately stood out, and he became my unofficial speaking coach, helping me refine my own presentation skills. Joe's transition from football to broadcasting and his expertise in delivering powerful messages have been an inspiration to me.

John O'Hurley—I first met the iconic actor turned spokesman, best known for his role as J. Peterman on *Seinfeld* on the set of *The X-Files* in Vancouver, and our connection only grew from there. We went on to co-host 2 infomercials together, where his wit and charm perfectly complemented my passion for pitching. And, as a finalist on *Dancing with the Stars*, John even indulged me with a dance! Working with such a talented and versatile performer has put a new spin on possibilities for ALL of us!

Joy Mangano—On the HSN set, Joy Mangano made history with her Miracle Mop and Huggable Hangers, later inspiring the Oscar-nominated film *Joy*, starring Jennifer Lawrence. As 2 Long Island girls who rose in the world of pitching, we share a deep appreciation for determination and innovation. Joy's journey from idea to impact is a true inspiration.

Ken Kerry—We collaborated on a variety of infomercial productions through Script to Screen, working closely with his wife and creative partner, Barb Kerry. The best team bringing a range of direct-response shows from concept to camera, combining strong scripting, smart structure, and confident on-air delivery. Ken had a gift for creating clarity in the chaos of production, keeping teams focused and shows moving forward. He represents a prolific period of creativity, momentum, and hands-on execution during the golden era of long-form television.

Kevin Harrington—In the early 90s, I was fortunate to team up with Kevin, a pioneer in the infomercial world and one of the original sharks on *Shark Tank*. Together, we created over a dozen infomercials, shaping the industry and launching careers for stars like Kim Kardashian, Chef Robert Irvine, and Montel Williams. Kevin and his brother Tim welcomed me into their world, bringing me to Florida to pitch products, create shows, and build a lifelong friendship. Their belief in me not only shaped my career but left an indelible mark on my heart.

Lee Majors—Pitching the "Bionic Ear, hearing aid" was one of my most unforgettable shows. I got to team up with the iconic, original *Six Million Dollar Man*. With his legendary status and my passion for pitching, we created a dynamic duo that had everyone tuning in. From fitness to hearing aids, if there's one thing I've learned, it's that pitching isn't about the product—it's about the story you tell. And trust me, with Lee Majors by my side, this was a story worth hearing!

Mindy Grossman (HSN CEO 2006–2017)—Working with Mindy was a masterclass in visionary leadership. During her tenure, she transformed the shopping channel into a lifestyle retail powerhouse. Under her guidance, I launched SpinGym and my empowering clothing line, Love My Body. Her belief in my vision and her unmatched ability to connect products with millions proved that a single, powerful pitch can create a movement.

Ron Popeil—He was an American inventor, marketing personality, and founder of the direct response marketing company Ronco. Ron's most famous infomercial was the Showtime Rotisserie, and he coined the phrase "Set it, and forget it!" and popularized the phrase "But wait, there's more!" on television as early as the mid-1950s. His mentorship and passion for pitching were unparalleled, but the craziest part is it turns out that Ron and I are related, second cousins by marriage… so pitching might just run in the family after all!

Tara Borakos—One of the most talented infomercial producers I've ever worked with. From health and beauty to fitness, she masterfully created shows I had the privilege to host, turning concepts into captivating on-air experiences. Her eye for detail, ability to shape compelling stories, and talent for connecting products to viewers set her apart in a league of her own.

Tim Harrington—We collaborated on multiple direct-response television campaigns including Top Chef University. In fact, Tim and his brother, Kevin (Shark Tank) were my first infomercial producers and introduced me to life in Florida. Known for his behind the scenes mastery of infomercial strategy and execution, Tim has played a pivotal role in shaping successful long-form television offers. Our work together reflects an era where strong storytelling, precise scripting, and on-camera authority determined success. Tim's ability to translate an idea from script to screen helped elevate products into nationally recognized brands… truly a special man!~

Tom Jourden—From the moment I met him on set, I knew I was working alongside a true pro. With his razor-sharp wit, smooth delivery, and an uncanny ability to make any product shine, Tom brought a level of ease and charisma that made co-hosting effortless. We partnered on several high-performing infomercials, and every shoot with him felt like magic—because it was. Tom stands out as the real deal, effortlessly engaging, endlessly professional, and unforgettable on camera.

Vince Offer—Hands down one of the best pitchmen ever. I spent many afternoons chatting with Vince, breaking down what makes a $100-Million-dollar offer. With his quirky, high-energy style, Vince turned a simple cleaning cloth into a household name, generating millions in sales with the ShamWow. The secret? It's more than just a great product; it's mastering the art of pitching with precision, confidence, and a touch of fun.

To really enjoy this era of infomercials you have to watch them! I've included some never-before-seen, behind-the-curtain footage—enjoy!

Scan the QR Code and go to the Resource Center (Chapter I).

J

"A job gives you a paycheck.
A pitch gives you freedom."
—Forbes Riley

CHAPTER J: Job

Job (noun): *A task, role, or work performed in exchange for payment, responsibility, or fulfillment.*

A job isn't just something you do to pay the bills; it's where you spend the majority of your waking hours. Whether you love what you do or feel stuck in a dead-end grind, your job has the power to shape your confidence, your self-worth, and even your identity.

But here's the truth: *A job should never just be about collecting a paycheck.* Your work should align with your values, challenge you to grow, and make you feel like your contributions matter. The people who thrive in their careers aren't just those with the best degrees or the most experience; they're the ones who know how to pitch themselves, their ideas, and their value.

Every job is a pitch. From the moment you send your first résumé, to the day you walk into a meeting and ask for a promotion, to the way you show up and lead in your workplace—*you are pitching.*

Jordan, a marketing manager, believed that hard work and dedication were enough to advance his career. He consistently met deadlines, delivered results, and assumed that his efforts would eventually be recognized. But after years of being overlooked for promotions and bigger opportunities, he realized that simply keeping his head down wasn't enough; something had to change. Hesitant to come across as pushy or ungrateful, he decided to take my *Pitch Like a Pro* training to learn how to communicate his values and aspirations with confidence and clarity. Recently, he reached out to share that after applying what he learned, he finally had a breakthrough; his boss not only acknowledged his contributions but also rewarded him with the long-awaited promotion.

Jordan's story is proof that mastering your pitch isn't just about selling a product; just check out what he recently wrote to me:

"Thank you! I finally got the promotion to head of marketing that I long deserved. You shattered everything I thought I knew about pitching. I always thought it was just for salespeople. But now I understand that I've been pitching every single day, whether it's in meetings, getting my boss to approve a project, or just speaking up in a way that makes people listen. Before, I felt invisible. Now, my ideas land, my confidence is higher, and for the first time, my boss sees me as a leader. Your training isn't just about pitching, it's about unlocking your full communication potential."

Jordan's story highlights something critical: your job isn't just about what you do, it's about how you present what you do. And if you don't know how to pitch yourself, someone else will take the opportunities meant for you. Think about it. Your entire professional journey is built on pitches:

- **Your résumé is your first pitch.** It's how you position yourself before they ever meet you.
- **Your interview is your next pitch.** You're selling your skills, experience, and why they should hire you.
- **Your everyday interactions at work are pitches.** You're constantly advocating for your ideas, your value, and your career growth.
- **Your raise or promotion is a pitch.** You're persuading leadership that you've earned that next level.
- **Your leadership is a pitch.** If you're in management, you're constantly pitching a vision, motivating your team, and earning their trust.

The problem? Most people never learn how to pitch themselves in a way that makes them unforgettable.

Instead, they assume that hard work alone will get them ahead. But here's the reality: *opportunities don't go to the most qualified—they go to the most visible and the most persuasive*.

Pitching is the single most important skill in your career, whether you realize it or not. It's the difference between blending in and standing out, between being overlooked and becoming indispensable. When you walk into an interview, your pitch is what makes an employer stop scanning résumés and say, "You're the one we've been looking for." In meetings, it's what gets your ideas heard instead of drowned out by louder voices. It's the tool that turns skepticism into belief, hesitation into action, and a no into a yes.

But pitching is more than just persuasion; it's positioning. The way you pitch yourself at work doesn't just determine the opportunities you get; it shapes how people perceive you. A strong pitch makes your boss see you as a leader before you even have the title. It's how you communicate your value, not just in words, but in confidence, clarity, and conviction. The people who rise aren't always the smartest or the most experienced; they're the ones who know how to articulate their worth, rally support, and present their ideas in a way that gets others to buy in. If you can't pitch yourself, you won't stand out. And if you don't stand out, you'll never move up.

- **Be clear on what you bring to the table.** Don't just say, "I work in marketing." Instead you might say, "I support the company by growing the brand and increasing revenue through creative storytelling and strategic campaigns."
- **Be confident in your value.** Don't downplay your achievements. Own them. Instead of, "I was just part of the team that launched that project," say, "I played a key role in launching that project, and we saw a 30% increase in engagement because of it."

- Make it about them. Whether you're pitching in an interview or asking for a promotion, always tie it back to the company's goals. Instead of, "I want a raise because I've been working really hard," say, "Over the past year, I've helped grow our department's revenue by 25%. I'd love to discuss aligning my compensation with the value I'm bringing to the company."

The second you learn how to advocate for yourself, doors open that you never even knew existed. Because if you don't believe in your own value, how can you expect anyone else to?

To bring these strategies to life, let's explore how they work in practice through a few scenarios.

Scenario 1: Pitching a New Project

You have an idea to streamline a workflow, but you need your boss's approval.

- *Understand Your Audience:* Define what your boss's priorities are and tailor your pitch to show how the project aligns with them.
- *Practice Emotional Engagement:* Share a quick story or example of how this workflow issue has created challenges, then explain how your idea solves it.

Scenario 2: Aligning Your Team Around a Goal

You're leading a project and need everyone's buy-in.

- *Be Personable:* Start by acknowledging everyone's hard work and finding common ground about the importance of the goal.
- *Clarity Is Key:* Clearly outline the steps to achieve the goal and how each team member's role contributes to the bigger picture.

Scenario 3: Asking for a Raise

You've been consistently exceeding expectations and feel it's time to discuss a raise. Using the strategies:

- *Focus on Shared Goals:* Begin by framing the discussion around your contributions to the company's success. "I'd like to discuss how my work has helped achieve [specific outcomes] and how we can align my compensation with that value."
- *Craft Your Message with Precision:* Be clear and specific about your request. "Based on my achievements and market research, I'd like to propose an increase of X% to reflect my contributions."

Your career is one continuous pitch.

Every job interview, every performance review, every leadership opportunity, it all hinges on how effectively you communicate your value. Hard work alone won't guarantee success. Talent alone won't open doors. The ones who rise aren't just the most capable; they're the ones who master the art of making their worth undeniable. They don't wait for recognition; they command it. They don't hope for opportunities; they create them.

So, what's next for you? A promotion? A raise? A leadership role you know you're ready for? More importantly, how will you pitch yourself to make it happen? That answer could change everything. And now, you have the tools to turn possibility into reality.

Step up. Speak out. Own your voice and pitch yourself for the success you deserve.

"An investment in knowledge pays the best interest."
—Benjamin Franklin

CHAPTER K: Knowledge

Knowledge (noun): *Facts, information, and skills acquired by a person through experience or education; the theoretical or practical understanding of a subject.*

I've always believed that knowledge is everywhere, not just in the pages of a textbook. When my kids were in grade school, I traveled internationally for business to places like China, Italy, and Germany on a regular basis. I grappled with the decision of whether to bring them along or keep them focused on their classes. Then, a dear friend gave me advice I'll never forget: "You should never let school get in the way of a good education." In that moment, I realized that true knowledge stretches far beyond the walls of any classroom.

School teaches you the basics, but the real lessons, the ones that truly shape your life, come from the experiences you dive into, the mistakes you grow from, and the things you learn along the way. It's when you step out of your comfort zone, take risks, and say yes to new opportunities that the magic happens. Formal education lays the groundwork, but it's the learning you actively pursue that truly transforms your life.

One of the most important lessons I learned came when I trained in martial arts after getting mugged. I started like everyone else with a white belt, the mark of a beginner, and gradually worked my way to a black belt. My instructor once taught me a powerful lesson: when a master's black belt wears thin and begins to fray, it reveals the white belt underneath. This simple realization taught me that even when you are the best, you will always be a student at your roots.

This concept became one of the core principles I teach about pitching because it's a skill that requires learning, practice, and dedication to truly master.

Most professions, from personal trainers to doctors, lawyers, and teachers, require ongoing education to stay current as their fields grow and evolve. Entrepreneurship, however, doesn't come with a clear roadmap of continual education. There's a wealth of options that can provide guidance and education such as courses, masterminds, and mentors. But the challenge lies in choosing the ones that will have the greatest impact.

Here are 5 strategies to grow your knowledge base every day:

1. **Be Curious.** The desire to explore and understand something new is the core of curiosity. Approaching new ideas with an open mind and a willingness to explore, rather than judge, creates endless opportunities to grow. Embracing curiosity with genuine interest will become your greatest ally in mastering the art of the pitch. Developing this as a habit will be essential for your growth.

2. **Read Daily.** One of the most effective ways to build your knowledge and stay ahead is reading. Whether it's a physical book, an e-book, or an article, dedicating even a few minutes each day allows you to absorb new ideas, gain valuable insights, and broaden your perspective. The power of reading remains unmatched in helping you grow and refine your expertise.

3. **Seek Out Mentors and Experts.** Connecting with experienced professionals in your field or areas of interest can significantly accelerate your growth. Mentors provide valuable insights, guidance, and shortcuts to success that you might not discover on your own. Build these relationships by attending workshops, webinars, or networking events where you can learn directly from those who have already walked the path you're pursuing.

4. **Learn by Doing.** There's no substitute for practical experience. Apply what you're discovering by testing new strategies, refining your skills, and observing the results. This could be through live pitching, experimenting with marketing techniques, or even starting side projects that let you test in real time.

5. **Embrace Mistakes.** Embrace your mistakes as the powerful stepping stones they are! In the past, failure was something to fear but today, every misstep is a lesson in disguise. For entrepreneurs, each awkward pitch, every stumble, and even the smallest setback is a chance to sharpen your skills, refine your strategies, and become more effective. Instead of dreading failure, welcome it as your greatest teacher.

"I have not failed. I've just found 10,000 ways that won't work." —Thomas Edison

Edison understood something crucial about knowledge: every failure was a lesson, every setback a stepping stone. The same principles apply to pitching. Every time you fall short, you're refining your approach and getting closer to your goal. The key is resilience: learning, adjusting, and coming back stronger.

By combining these strategies, you create a robust, dynamic learning environment that continually expands your knowledge and equips you to handle the challenges of entrepreneurship.

Throughout my career, I've gained wisdom that can only come from hands-on experience, being in the right place at the right time, and taking bold action. Now, it's my mission to pass that on, to leave a legacy that empowers you to pitch with purpose and confidence.

I think of knowledge like planting seeds. When you put them in the ground, you water them and tend to them, and over time they will blossom. Just like some seeds sprout faster than others, different pitching skills require varying amounts of time and attention to flourish. Some will take root quickly, while others need more care and nurturing. If you want a lush and diverse garden of pitch mastery, you need patience and skills to tend to your knowledge, so it can blossom.

Remember: Stay curious, stay hungry, and never stop learning. Because in this game, knowledge isn't just power; it's your ultimate advantage.

If you're ready to grow...

Scan the QR Code to explore the free *Pitch Secrets A to Z* Resource Center (Chapter K).

*"A lead isn't just a contact,
it's a conversation waiting
to become a connection."
—Forbes Riley*

CHAPTER L: Leads

Leads (noun): *A group of people who are or could be i nterested in the product or service you sell.*

One of the most critical parts of any business is acquiring customers. You could have the best product or service in the world, but if no one knows about it or is buying it, what's the point? Leads are the lifeblood of your business; they're the people who show interest in what you're offering.

My dad was an eccentric inventor, part Willy Wonka, part Doc Brown (from *Back to the Future),* with a spark of childlike wonder that never faded. His garage was a living laboratory, shelves overflowing with wires, gears, and half-finished contraptions. In one corner sat *The Thinker Blinker*, his version of an early computer, its mismatched lights flickering as if it might suddenly spring to life. Across the room, a homemade Batmobile, sculpted from half a garbage can, a lawn mower engine, and layers of paper-mâché, ready for imaginary adventures. The air always smelled of sawdust, solder, and pure imagination. His creations were magical, whimsical bursts of genius that sadly, few outside our family ever got to see or experience.

One day, he turned to me and asked,

"Kiddo, how do I get my inventions out into the world?"

I looked at him, wide-eyed, and replied,

"Dad, I have no idea. I'm 8 years old."

Sadly when he died, all his dreams died with him. That moment stayed with me and became the driving force behind why I do what I do.

I've dedicated much of my career to bringing inventors' products to life on television, from home shopping to infomercials. Along the way, I learned that sharing your ideas and gaining traction all come down to how you communicate your ideas in your pitch.

The ability to generate leads, getting people interested in your offer, starts with one thing: **How well you communicate your ideas**.

Because when you speak with clarity and conviction, people don't just hear you; they *feel* you. And when they feel you, they follow you. That's how leads become relationships, and relationships become results.

Everything we've covered so far has been building this framework. Communication isn't just about speaking; it's about connecting, influencing, and inspiring action. Each principle you've learned up to this point is part of that process:

> **B—Believe in yourself and your product.**
> **C—Confidently close when you meet someone.**
> **D—Demonstrate your value.**
> **E—Effectively engage others into your vision.**

All of these build the foundation for lead generation, because generating leads isn't about chasing people; it's about inspiring them. It's about turning curiosity into commitment.

Lead generation isn't just about finding people; it's about inspiring them to believe in your idea, connect with your product, and ultimately take action.

In order to turn a lead into a customer you need to understand the foundation of what a lead is and how to acquire one.

Leads can show up in different ways in your business. They may follow you on social media, visit your website, or engage in conversation with you. The types of leads you'll interact with will vary depending on how familiar they are with you, what you offer, and how much they know, like, and trust you.

Leads Fall into 3 Categories:

- **Cold leads** are people who have never heard of you before; they may come across a post of yours, see an ad you put out, or hear about you through a referral. These leads require the most nurturing as they are strangers. Think of them like a first date: it's all about making a strong impression and clearly showcasing your value.

- **Warm leads** are people who have seen you before, are familiar with what you are up to, and have potentially interacted with you. They're like friends who haven't been to your house yet; they know you, but they need a compelling reason to take that next step and engage further.

- **Hot leads** are people who know you well, like you, and want exactly what you offer, but haven't bought from you yet. They're on the verge of purchasing, but they just need that final push to transform their interest into action.

Getting in front of new leads is the first step, and it doesn't have to be complicated. Your approach will depend on your preferences, expertise, and the nature of your business. The key is consistency, showing up regularly in places where your potential prospects are already spending their time.

5 Proven Strategies for Acquiring and Keeping Leads:

1. **Leverage Social Media:** Consistency is key; don't just post and ghost! Think of your profiles as your digital storefront or business card. Engage with comments, share valuable content, and be present. Keep it fun, inviting, and intentional to your business to show people who you are and what you offer.

2. **Free Resources or Lead Magnets:** Provide something valuable, such as an e-book, checklist, webinar, or free trial, in exchange for contact information. A well-designed lead magnet not only captures interest but also builds trust and positions you as an expert.

3. **Utilize the Power of Networking:** Whether in-person or virtual, events provide a prime opportunity to meet potential leads. Go to your local Chamber of Commerce, participate in groups online, and get into social clubs. You can't sit around and wait for the phone to ring! The focus here is on giving value first; don't just show up asking for business. Invest in building relationships before you need them.

4. **Collaborate with Others in Your Industry:** Partner with complementary businesses, influencers, or industry experts to co-host events, create joint content, or run giveaways. Cross-promotion and referrals allow you to tap into new audiences who already trust and value the person recommending you, making it easier to build credibility and connection.

5. **Have a Good Follow-Up Strategy:** It is a LOT easier (and less expensive!) to retain a customer than to acquire a new one! Create a system for regular check-ins, whether through email, phone calls, or personal notes. The fortune is in the follow-up!

Leads are not just names on a list; they represent opportunities to create meaningful relationships and lasting impact. By implementing the strategies outlined you're not just acquiring leads; you're building trust, delivering value, and positioning yourself as the solution your prospects are seeking.

Remember, your goal isn't to simply sell; it's to serve. Long-term success in business isn't about chasing onetime sales; it's about building lifelong relationships.

As Zig Ziglar wisely said, *"Stop selling. Start helping."* When you shift your focus to genuinely helping others, you'll find that leads are no longer something to chase; they're a natural outcome of your dedication, passion, and service.

That's why I always say: treat every lead like they're your only lead. Whether you're responding to a social media comment or meeting someone at a networking event, give them your full attention. Make them feel heard. Show them you care about solving their problem, not just making a sale.

Your pitch is the bridge between having someone's attention and earning their business. Be consistent, be authentic, and always be prepared because you never know when that next conversation could turn into your biggest opportunity.

Here's the real secret: the best leads often come from happy customers who sing your praises. Focus on serving your current leads exceptionally well, and they'll become your greatest advocates, generating valuable referrals. And remember, it's always more cost-effective to nurture existing customers than to constantly search for new ones.

With this mindset, you're not just building a business—you're creating a legacy.

"Whether you think you can, or you think you can't—you're right."

—Henry Ford

CHAPTER M: Mindset

Mindset (noun): *The established set of beliefs and attitudes that shape thinking, behavior, and decisions.*

Henry Ford, the visionary behind the Ford Motor Company, understood the immense power of mindset. Your mind is either your greatest ally or your biggest obstacle. If you believe you can do something, you will find a way to make it happen and your brain gets to work finding solutions. But if you believe you can't, you've shut the door before it could open and you'll sabotage your efforts before you've even started.

Thoughts and beliefs shape your reality. That's the power of mindset; it drives every decision, every action, and ultimately, every result. Whether you're pitching an idea, launching a business, or striving to reach the next level, your mindset forms the foundation on which everything else is built.

This truth comes to life in one of my favorite and most iconic stories ever told: *The Wizard of Oz*. More than a magical journey, it's a profound metaphor for self-belief, inner strength, and the bravery to take action. Dorothy, the Scarecrow, the Tin Man, and the Cowardly Lion are driven on a journey by the belief that the Mighty Wizard of Oz can solve their problems. Dorothy wants to go home, the Cowardly Lion seeks courage, the Scarecrow desires a brain, and the Tin Man longs for a heart. They believe their dreams hinge on finding this Wizard, an all-powerful figure who can make their wishes come true.

However, as their adventure unfolds, something remarkable happens. Through their challenges and victories, each character unknowingly demonstrates the very qualities they thought they were missing. The Scarecrow devises clever plans, the Tin Man shows deep compassion, and the Cowardly Lion exhibits incredible bravery. Dorothy leads the way with resilience and determination.

In the end, the Wizard doesn't grant them anything they didn't already have. Instead, he reveals the truth: their perceived limitations were merely a matter of mindset. Glinda, the Good Witch, solidifies this lesson when she tells Dorothy, "You've always had the power inside of you."

This story has always inspired me because it clearly illustrates that your mindset shapes not only how you see yourself, but what you're capable of achieving. When you believe you are lacking, you create barriers that hold you back. But when you shift your mindset to recognize your strengths, you unlock the power to overcome challenges and achieve your goals.

Each character's journey mirrors the process of self-discovery and personal growth. Their transformation didn't come from the Wizard's tricks or Glinda's magic; it came from within. The Scarecrow's intellect, the Tin Man's heart, and the Lion's courage were always there; they just needed to give themselves permission to embrace these qualities.

As children, studies estimate that we hear the word "no" an estimated 400 times a day during our early development. By the time we reach age 18, we may have heard "no" or other negative statements (e.g., "You can't," "Don't do that") tens of thousands of times, far more frequently than hearing affirmations like "yes" or "you can."

Over time, these limitations build real barriers and condition us to ask for outside permission at every step of the way. The truth is, no one else's approval can determine your future. We clearly learned from the Wizard of Oz that the permission you seek must come from within.

It's time to flip the script and reclaim your power. The ability to take bold steps and embrace your full potential starts with recognizing what's holding you back. Are self-doubts keeping you from taking action? Check all that apply:

- ❑ **Fear of Failure**
  You worry about the possibility of failing and what others will think if you don't succeed. This fear can create hesitation and prevent action.
- ❑ **Imposter Syndrome**
  You believe that you're not qualified or capable, despite your achievements, often fueled by comparisons to others and the fear of being "found out" as undeserving.
- ❑ **Perfectionism**
  You relentlessly believe everything must be flawless before taking action, often leaving you stuck in preparation mode, trapping you in a cycle of overthinking and delaying your dreams, while the opportunity to grow and succeed slips by.
- ❑ **Analysis Paralysis**
  You overthink every detail and wait for the "perfect plan" which stops you from starting. You tend to focus on all the things that need to happen rather than just taking the first step.
- ❑ **External Validation**
  You feel the need for approval or support from others before moving forward, whether it's family, mentors, or peers, before feeling confident enough to take the next step.
- ❑ **Fear of Success**
  You are scared of the responsibilities, expectations, or lifestyle changes that achieving your goals might bring. This fear can quietly hold you back, creating hesitation as you grapple with the weight of stepping into your full potential.
- ❑ **Lack of Resources**
  You complain about not having enough time, money, or connections. You believe that success requires perfect conditions, which rarely exist.
- ❑ **Fear of Not Being Enough**
  You doubt your abilities, worth, or qualifications, worrying that you'll fall short no matter how much effort you put in. This fear holds you back from taking risks, makes you second-guess yourself, and leaves you stuck in a cycle of self-doubt.

If any of these resonate with you, you are not alone.

Every entrepreneur, dreamer, and visionary faces a variety of these same fears. Doubts and uncertainty are part of the journey, but what matters is how you confront them, reframe them, and transform them into the driving force that propels you forward.

The good news? You can rewire your brain to overcome limiting beliefs, and one of the most effective tools is the use of affirmations.

Affirmations tap into the power of the subconscious mind, helping to shift thought patterns, build confidence, and create alignment between one's beliefs and actions. When practiced regularly, they become a tool for fostering a positive, growth-oriented mindset.

One of the most effective affirmations I've used to achieve my goals and create the life I envisioned comes from the power of permission.

Once you grant yourself permission, you'll see doors open where there used to be walls. You'll start to notice opportunities in places you never thought possible. That's the magic of mindset: it doesn't change the world around you, but it changes how you engage with the world.

The Forbes Riley you know today was built on the foundation of one powerful affirmation I repeat daily, silencing self-doubt and creating a life beyond my wildest dreams. It's straightforward yet incredibly powerful:

"I hereby grant myself permission to:

> *stop playing small, to pitch my ideas, gifts, and value with confidence, knowing they create impact, abundance, and transformation for others and to finally step past the 'what ifs' to claim the success, freedom, and joy I've always known is mine."*

Here are examples of how to transform your fears into permission and change the narrative, turning self-doubt into empowering beliefs.

Fear of Failure	**I hereby grant myself permission** to embrace mistakes as part of the journey and see failure as an opportunity to learn and grow.
Imposter Syndrome	**I hereby grant myself permission to** own my strengths and trust I am worthy of success.
Perfectionism	**I hereby grant myself permission to** take messy, imperfect action and trust that I'll figure things out along the way, to not let the perfect ruin the good.
Analysis Paralysis	**I hereby grant myself permission to** focus on one step at a time and let go of overwhelm.
External Validation	**I hereby grant myself permission to** trust my own judgment and move forward with confidence, without needing approval from others.
Fear of Success	**I hereby grant myself permission to** step into the life I desire and embrace all the responsibilities it brings.
Lack of Resources	**I hereby grant myself permission to** start where I am, with what I have, building success through creativity, trusting that abundance will flow.
Fear of Not Being Enough	**I hereby grant myself permission to** believe that I am enough, just as I am, even in my imperfection. I choose to embrace my flaws and move forward with courage and self-acceptance.

By repeating affirmations, you rewire your mind to embrace empowering beliefs that inspire action and foster growth. This shifts your focus from negative thoughts to positive possibilities, countering the brain's natural tendency to dwell on fears and problems.

Here's how to bring this practice to life:

Step 1: Write Your Affirmation

Take a moment to reflect on the action or goal you've been hesitating to pursue. Write this empowerment statement in this format:

"I hereby grant myself permission to

____

____

____."

(Fill in the blank with what has been holding you back from achieving success.)

Step 2: Put It Where You'll See It

Place your affirmation where it can't be missed: your bathroom mirror, a sticky note on your desk, or as the wallpaper on your phone. This keeps it top of mind every day.

Step 3: Practice

Speak your affirmation aloud with conviction every day. Address the version of yourself that knows you are worthy, capable, and ready to achieve greatness. Begin each morning by granting yourself permission, and repeat it anytime insecurity starts to creep in.

Step 4: Repeat Until It Feels Real

At first, it might feel awkward or forced, but don't stop. Repetition is key. With each day, your brain begins to believe what you tell it, rewiring negative thought patterns into empowering ones.

Step 5: Follow Through with Action

Affirmations are just the beginning. Take one small step toward your goal immediately after repeating your empowerment statement. Action builds momentum and reinforces the belief that you are capable.

Example Process in Action:

1. **Write:** "I hereby grant myself permission to be confident."
2. **Place:** Put it on your bathroom mirror.
3. **Say:** Each morning, look in the mirror and repeat it aloud.
4. **Act:** Head to your closet, choose an outfit that makes you feel empowered, and put on a smile to start your day with positive intention.

I've created a tool to help you turn permission into action: the Permission Card. This is your personal reminder that you don't need anyone else's approval to chase your dreams, break free from limitations, and live the life you've always wanted.

Your mindset is the invisible helm steering every decision, action, and outcome. But belief alone isn't enough—give yourself permission to act on that belief. Mindset isn't just about thinking differently; it's about freeing yourself from the internal barriers that hold you back.

When you grant yourself permission to think, feel, and move in alignment with your goals, previously imagined blocks begin to fall away. In that space, meaningful progress isn't just possible—it's inevitable.

Ready to claim your permission card?

Scan the QR Code and head over to the Resource Center (Chapter M) to get your Permission Card to start giving yourself the green light to thrive.

The power to change your life is already within you, this is just your first step to claiming it.

N

"Words don't just describe your world; they build it. Master your language, and you master your results."
—Forbes Riley

CHAPTER N: Neuro-Linguistic Programming (NLP)

Neuro-Linguistic Programming (NLP) (noun):
A methodology that explores the connection between language, thoughts, and behaviors to help individuals communicate effectively, overcome limitations, and achieve their goals.

I've always been fascinated by the power of the mind, but a pivotal moment in my acting career brought this curiosity to life. I was cast in a one-woman show, *The Search for Signs of Intelligent Life in the Universe*, written by Tony Award–winning comedian Lily Tomlin and her partner, Jane Wagner. It was a dream role, but with a monumental challenge. I got to play 15 distinct characters without costume or set changes. Every transition relied solely on my voice, body language, and presence. And if that wasn't enough, I had to memorize 250 pages of dialogue, word for word.

At first, I was confident in my acting abilities, but the sheer volume of material left me mentally blocked. I could not retain the lines, no matter what I did. At one point I even asked the director to replace me because I didn't want to embarrass myself or the production.

That's when everything changed.

The director introduced me to a hypnotherapist who taught me how to access, store, and retrieve information by working with my subconscious mind.

Suddenly, everything clicked.

Here I am with Lily Tomlin performing just a few of the many characters I brought to life from *The Search for Signs of Intelligent Life in the Universe.*

I memorized every word, performed for 6 months straight without missing a beat, and discovered something far more powerful than acting technique: *The mind can be trained. The brain is programmable.* This discovery sparked my lifelong passion for Neuro-Linguistic Programming (NLP).

The experience changed my life, sparking a deep fascination with how the human brain works and its ability to be trained and optimized. This curiosity led me to discover a system that allows you to access the subconscious part of your brain, enhancing effective communication and the ability to influence behavior through the power of language.

From the moment I attended my first training, I was hooked and eventually became a certified practitioner. NLP didn't just change the way I thought about acting and memorization; it transformed my approach to communication. It became the foundation of how I connect, pitch ideas, close deals, and nurture personal relationships.

What is NLP?

Let's set the record straight. Neuro-Linguistic Programming might sound like intimidating scientific jargon, but at its heart, it's a framework for understanding how your brain processes language, how words influence your thoughts, and how those thoughts shape your behavior and interactions.

NLP empowers you to communicate in ways that captivate, connect, and inspire. It's the core reason behind my success as a pitcher, because so often, we get stuck on the words we say, forgetting they're just one piece of the puzzle. True connection and impact come from the entire package: your tone, body language, and how you make people feel when you deliver your message.

With NLP, you're creating a symphony in your pitch that draws people in effortlessly. If you've ever been captivated by a pitch that left you wanting more, chances are the person pitching was using NLP, whether they knew it or not. It's the secret sauce that makes your message resonate, helps you connect on an emotional level, and guides your audience to see themselves in the solution you're offering.

NLP offers a range of tools but there are 3 foundational techniques that stand out when it comes to your ability to elevate your pitch. These methods aren't just effective; they're practical, simple to learn, and applicable to everyday life.

3 NLP Techniques to Elevate Your Pitch

1. Anchoring

Anchoring is a process that connects a specific cue (such as a word, gesture, or touch) to a desired emotional state, enabling you to instantly access feelings like confidence, motivation, or calmness whenever you need them.

Applications for Anchoring:

Overcoming Self-Doubt

Scenario: When you're feeling anxious or unmotivated before a pitch, grab your earbuds and play a specific song that always energizes or focuses you. Over time, just hearing the opening notes sparks a surge of enthusiasm.

Why It Works: The music acts as an anchor, linking those sounds to a state of energy and drive. This quick mood boost helps you tackle your tasks with renewed focus and positivity.

Pitching with Confidence

Scenario: You're about to do your sales pitch on stage or give a big presentation, and that familiar wave of nervousness starts to creep in. Instead of letting stage fright take over, you create an anchor of confidence by pressing your thumb and forefinger together while vividly recalling a moment when you felt unstoppable.

Why It Works: This simple physical action, practiced over time, becomes a "trigger" for shifting your anxiety to assurance.

By intentionally creating anchors, you can tap into emotional states that enhance your performance, giving you the tools to take control of your mindset. It allows you to show up empowered, focused, and ready to seize the moments that matter most.

By creating a physical or mental anchor, you can instantly step into your most persuasive state the moment you open your mouth. Instead of hoping you'll "feel ready," you trigger readiness.

2. Reframing

Framing refers to the way we perceive and interpret situations, events, or communication. It's the mental "lens" or "context" through which we view the world. Your frame influences how you think, feel, and respond to what's happening around you.

Reframing is the process of deliberately changing that lens or context to shift your perception, often transforming negative or limiting beliefs into empowering, constructive ones. It's a methodology for creating better outcomes by seeing a situation differently.

Applications for Reframing:

From Failure to Feedback

Old Frame: "I failed at pitching my product; I'm not cut out for this."

Reframe: "This pitch taught me what doesn't work, giving me valuable insights for my next attempt."

Why It Works: Reframing transforms the emotional weight of failure into a learning opportunity, fostering resilience.

From Rejection to Redirection

Old Frame: "My pitch was rejected, and I lost the deal."

Reframe: "This wasn't the right fit, but now I know how to refine my approach and am excited to do it again. After all professional baseball players who make millions strike out ⅔ of the time and are still considered great!

Why It Works: Entrepreneurs learn to see rejection as a step closer to alignment with their ideal clients or partners.

Reframing is a powerful tool that enables you to see challenges from a fresh perspective, transforming setbacks into stepping stones for growth. By shifting your mindset, you can approach problems with resilience and clarity, unlocking solutions that once felt out of reach.

3. Future Pacing

Future pacing is a powerful NLP technique that allows you to vividly imagine yourself achieving a desired outcome. It works by guiding your mind to visualize a specific scenario where you have already succeeded, creating an emotional connection to that success. This mental rehearsal not only builds confidence but also ensures that new behaviors or beliefs feel natural and attainable.

One of the most valuable aspects of future pacing is the ability to anchor positive feelings to your visualization. Think of future pacing as a dress rehearsal for your dreams. For example, if you're preparing for a public speaking event, you might imagine yourself on stage, confidently delivering your message to an engaged audience.

In this mental scene, you hear the applause, see the attentive faces of the crowd, and feel a sense of accomplishment as you finish your speech.

Picture yourself breathing steadily, thinking clearly, and navigating the moment with ease and control. This practice creates a strong emotional connection to your desired outcome, making it easier to believe in and work toward.

Think of future pacing as a dress rehearsal for your dreams.

When you consistently imagine what you want, you align your thoughts, emotions, and actions with that vision, making it more likely to become your reality.

Future Pacing Your Pitches

- **"Imagine waking up tomorrow with absolute clarity on your message...** and knowing that every time you speak, people lean in, engage, and say YES to your offer."
- **"What would it feel like if...** in the next 90 days, you had the confidence to pitch on any stage, in any room, and close deals effortlessly?"
- **"Picture yourself 6 months from now...** standing on stage, delivering a pitch so powerful that investors are literally fighting to work with you."

Future Pacing for *Pitch Secrets A to Z*

- "**By the time you finish this book...** you'll have bulletproof pitches that attract clients, investors, and opportunities like never before."
- "**A year from now, you'll look back at today and realize**... this was the moment everything changed—the day you took control of your future."
- "**What would it feel like to know...** that you never have to 'wing it' again? That every pitch you give is clear, powerful, and persuasive?"

These 3 foundational techniques barely scratch the surface of NLP's transformative potential. Anchoring, reframing, and future pacing allow you to break through self-doubt and deliver with authenticity and impact. The better you understand the many different strategies, the more you will personally develop and connect better with your audience.

NLP isn't just about mastering language—it's about mastering states. Because the truth is, people don't buy your product, your service, or even your pitch. They buy the state you put them in. If you speak from fear, they feel hesitation. If you speak from certainty, they feel conviction. Anchoring, reframing, and language patterns give you the internal switches to control your emotional state, so you can transmit confidence, clarity, and charisma on demand. When your inner world is aligned, your outer words hit different.

But here's the catch: just like any skill, NLP mastery takes practice.

It's not enough to know about these techniques; you have to use them, refine them, and make them your own. The more you integrate NLP into your communication style, the more success you'll see, not just in pitching, but in every conversation you have. When you learn how to master your mind, everything else follows.

In the end, NLP gives you the edge most pitchers never have: the ability to speak to both the conscious and subconscious mind. When you master it, your pitch stops sounding like persuasion and starts feeling like truth.

That's why the best pitchers don't force the "yes." They create the mental environment where yes becomes inevitable. And when you can do that, you're not just pitching—you're transforming the way people think, feel, and decide.

Unlock the Skill That Changes Everything

If you're ready to break through limiting beliefs, become a more persuasive speaker, and build unstoppable confidence, NLP is the treasure chest you've been searching for.

This powerful approach helps you reshape your inner world so your outer results follow.

Scan the QR Code to access the Resource Center (Chapter N) and master the skill of NLP.

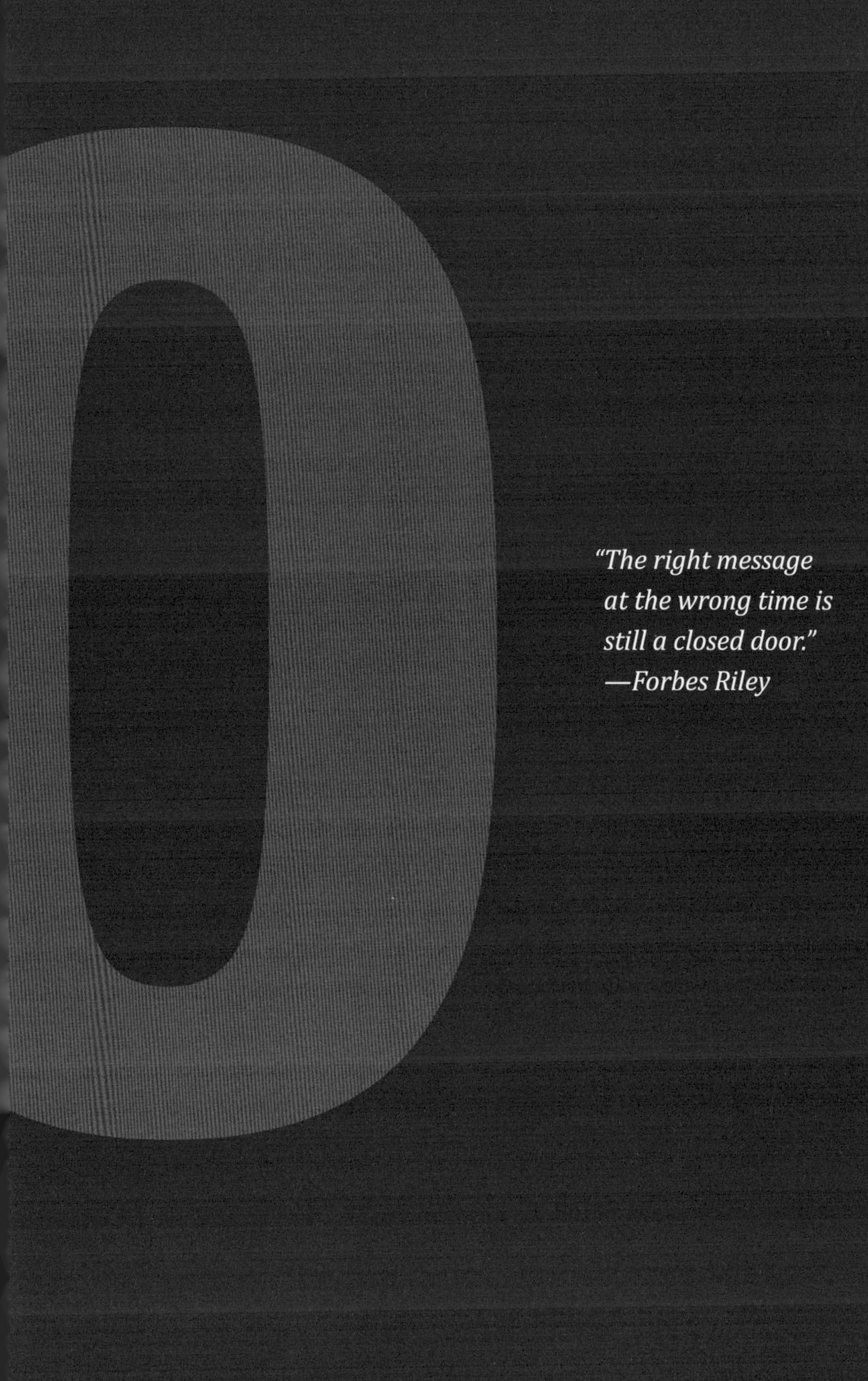

"The right message at the wrong time is still a closed door."
—Forbes Riley

CHAPTER O: Open Door

Open Door (noun): *The ability to recognize the right moment to pitch, when your audience is receptive, engaged, and ready to say yes.*

Opportunities are like doors. Some swing wide open, welcoming you inside. Others stay locked, no matter how hard you push. And sometimes, the biggest mistake people make isn't failing to walk through an open door—it's banging on the wrong one, wasting time and energy when something better is waiting just around the corner.

When it comes to pitching, an open door is more than just an opportunity; it's the difference between acceptance and rejection. Timing, awareness, and knowing when to step forward or step back is crucial. Too many people assume pitching is about persuasion, but that's only part of the equation. The real key? Recognizing when your prospect is receptive. If you push too soon, you're met with resistance. If you hesitate, the moment passes. Learning to recognize open doors is what separates those who struggle from those who succeed.

I see this mistake all the time. People pitch at the wrong time, to the wrong person, in the wrong way, and then wonder why they're facing rejection. They focus so much on what they're saying that they miss *when* they should be saying it. Pitching isn't just about delivering your message; it's about reading the room, feeling the energy, and stepping in when the door is open.

The Jump Rope Principle

Think back to childhood and the classic jump rope game: 2 kids swing the rope while a third waits for the perfect moment to jump in. If you mistime it, you get tangled up or smacked in the face. If you hesitate too long, the opportunity passes you by. But those who master the rhythm? They move effortlessly, knowing exactly when to step in.

That's how pitching works. If you push at the wrong time, you'll be met with resistance. You might have the best idea, the most valuable offer, but if your prospect isn't mentally, emotionally, and physically present, your pitch will fall flat. Ever talked to someone who's half-listening, scrolling on their phone, or distracted by something else? You might as well be talking to a brick wall.

A closed door isn't always locked forever, but if you keep banging on it, you'll irritate the person on the other side. Instead of forcing your way in, step back and observe. Is this the right moment? Is this person open to receiving what you're offering? If not, save yourself and them the discomfort of an awkward rejection.

Recognizing an Open Door

An open door doesn't announce itself with flashing lights. It's subtle. It's in the way someone leans in when you speak, the questions they ask, the curiosity in their voice. It's in their body language, their energy, the way they engage. When a door is open, your pitch isn't a disruption—it's a welcome opportunity.

So how do you recognize it? First, **listen more than you speak.** When you're passionate about what you're pitching, it's easy to get caught up in your own excitement. But real connection happens when you focus on what the other person is saying, not just waiting for your turn to talk. Ask a question. Pause. Let them speak. Pay attention to their responses. If the door is open, you'll feel it. If it's closed, pushing harder won't help.

Second, **watch for signals**. If you're talking and you notice the other person's eyes glazing over, their body shifting, or their attention drifting, that's a sign you're losing them. Instead of plowing ahead, take a step back. Re-engage them with a question, shift the conversation, or simply stop talking for a moment. Sometimes silence is more powerful than words.

Third, **set the stage** before you pitch. Have you ever started a conversation only to realize the person you're talking to is barely listening? Before you dive into your pitch, make sure the other person is present. Say something like, "Hey, I've got something really exciting to share with you. Let me know when you have a minute to focus on this. I think you'll love it." That simple setup creates an open door instead of forcing your way into a conversation that isn't ready for you.

One day, my brother-in-law, who I'd never been particularly close with, called me out of the blue. We saw each other at social events, exchanged polite conversation, but that was about it. He rang me up, voice filled with excitement, saying, *"I've got a tremendous opportunity for you! Let's meet for lunch."*

I told him, *"Listen, I'm running my own business. I'm not looking for another opportunity."* But he wouldn't take no for an answer. His urgency was so over-the-top that I finally agreed, more out of politeness than curiosity.

When we met for lunch, I was expecting something game-changing. And then he hit me with it: *"I just started working with a network marketing company. I want you to get involved. You could make an extra $10,000 a month!"*

Now, here's the problem. He wasn't making $10,000 a month. He wasn't even close. And worse, he hadn't been up front with me. If he had just led with honesty, *"Hey, I'm excited about this new business, and I'd love your support"* I probably would have bought something just to help him out. But instead, he attempted to *pitch* me without reading the room, without understanding if this was something I was open to or even interested in.

Now contrast that with another experience. My twin best friends, who I trust implicitly, called me up and said, *"We just got into a new travel network marketing company, and it's phenomenal. You get great discount prices at resorts, and we know how much you love to travel, plus we can take trips together. Would you be open to taking a look?"*

No pressure, no exaggerated income claims, just an open and honest conversation that aligned with what I was already passionate about, and they leveraged that.

Guess what? I signed up. And 5 years later, I'm still part of that company because they opened the door the *right way*.

The real takeaway? A pitch isn't won by the loudest voice, the flashiest offer, or even the best product. It's won by connection. By trust. By timing. If you don't read the room, you don't just risk losing the sale; you risk slamming the door shut before it ever has a chance to open.

Opportunities don't always announce themselves. Some doors swing wide open, some stay locked no matter how hard you push, and some are hidden in plain sight, waiting for you to notice. Your job isn't to force your way in; it's to sense when the moment is right, to step forward when the time comes, and to walk through with confidence.

Listen more than you speak. Observe what's happening in front of you. Pay attention to the small details most people overlook. And when the right door appears, don't hesitate.

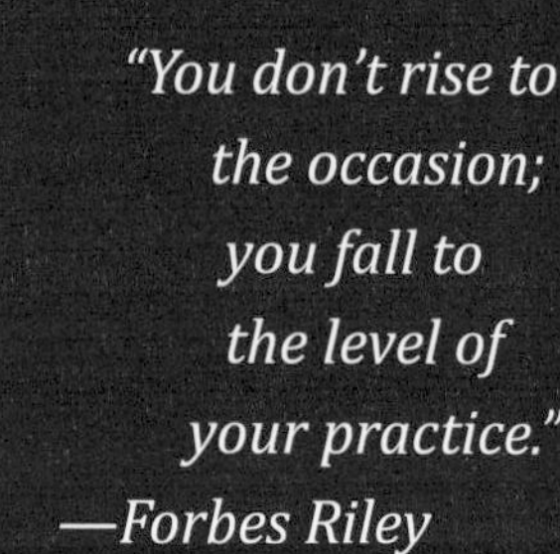

*"You don't rise to
the occasion;
you fall to
the level of
your practice."*
—Forbes Riley

CHAPTER P: Practice

Practice (noun): The deliberate repetition of actions and strategies to build confidence and enhance skills.

When I think back to my biggest wins, none of them happened by accident. They were the result of hours of practice and real-time adjustments. I learned to read my audience and adapt on the fly, pivoting within seconds to deliver a pitch that resonated. Every misstep, every challenge was a crash course in refining my pitch. Now, when people see me convert an unpolished pitch into something magical in minutes, they often ask, "How do you do that so fast?"

The answer? Decades of practice. Thousands of pitches. Repetition, over and over again.

Here's the thing: if you're new to pitching, cut yourself some slack. Every master was once a beginner. Those smooth, flawless pitches you see? They didn't happen overnight. They are the result of years of practice.

"You wouldn't take your first driving lesson on the freeway. Don't give your first pitch to your most important prospect."

Start small. Pitch to yourself. To a friend. To your pet if you have to. Every repetition builds confidence, skill, and intuition. No pitch is wasted when it becomes a lesson.

Mastery Requires Relentless Practice

Take Michael Jordan, one of the greatest athletes in history, for example. Everyone talks about his talent, but what they often overlook is the tireless hours he put in, even after he was already considered the best. He didn't just show up on game day; he obsessed over every detail, every shot, every mistake, long before the crowd ever saw him play.

I recently watched *The Last Dance* docuseries, and hearing Jordan himself describe his ruthless commitment to practice, teamwork, and constant improvement was eye-opening. It's a masterclass in what it truly takes to achieve mastery.

Jordan didn't coast on talent alone. He practiced harder than anyone on the court, constantly pushing himself to elevate his game. His success wasn't just due to athleticism; it was built on a foundation of hard work, dedication, and continuous refinement.

Jordan once said, "Talent alone doesn't make you great. Practice does." And that's the truth. When you see someone excel—whether it's in sports, business, or pitching—you're only witnessing the result of countless hours of practice behind the scenes. Success doesn't just "happen." It's earned through grit and consistent repetition.

If you're wondering how to practice pitching without the high-stakes pressure, here are 5 ways to sharpen your skills:

1. **Pitch to Yourself in Front of a Mirror:** Watch your body language and facial expressions. Do you look confident? Adjust as you go. Confidence is key in pitching, and a mirror can help you visualize how you come across to others, allowing you to make real-time adjustments.

2. **Pitch to Your Pet:** Yes, really! Your pet won't judge, and it helps you get comfortable hearing your own voice. Speaking to a pet reduces the fear of judgment, which allows you to focus on the words and tone, helping you build comfort with your delivery. Plus, pets are great listeners!

3. **Record Yourself:** Seeing yourself on video provides invaluable insights. You can analyze your performance from a neutral perspective, identifying areas where you might improve, like pacing, clarity, or tone. This is especially effective because it mimics the experience of being recorded during actual pitch situations.

4. **Ask Trusted Friends for Feedback:** Get honest feedback from those who will be candid but kind. They can offer a fresh perspective, pointing out areas where you may not notice any weaknesses. The combination of kind yet honest feedback can help refine your pitch and boost your confidence.

5. **Pitch to Strangers:** This is the most challenging but also the most effective method. Engage people who are waiting, whether they are in the park, in an airport, or standing in line. Ask them politely if you could practice your pitch. There is no obligation just a response and feedback. Strangers provide an unbiased perspective, giving you the ultimate test of how your pitch resonates.

Here's something most people don't realize about practice: It's not just about perfecting one pitch. It's about learning to read the room and adapt in real time. Every audience is different, and what works for one might fall flat with another.

When I pitch on QVC, I'm speaking to millions of people watching from their homes. They need to feel like I'm having a one-on-one conversation with them, sharing honest advice from a trusted friend. But when I pitch to corporate executives? That's a whole different game. They want data, results, and bottom-line impact.

Through practice, you'll learn to recognize these different audience types and adjust your approach:

- **The Analytical Audience:** They want facts, figures, and proof. Practice incorporating relevant data, 3rd-party endorsement, and concrete examples into your pitch.
- **The Emotional Buyers:** They make decisions based on feelings and personal connection. The best way to build authentic relationships with them is through storytelling.
- **The Skeptics:** They need extra reassurance and validation. Anticipate objections and address them proactively in your pitch before they arise. Have responses ready for common concerns, such as pricing, reliability, or return on investment.
- **The Quick Deciders:** They want the bottom line up front. Practice delivering your key points concisely and early. Be clear about your call to action and make it easy to avoid frustration.

The secret is to practice shifting between these styles until it becomes second nature. Start with your core message, then practice delivering it in different ways. It's like having multiple pitches in your arsenal; you can pull out the right one at the right moment.

But let's be clear: practice isn't glamorous. It's not about perfection; it's about repetition and refinement. It's about building confidence and preparing for that moment when the door swings open, and you step through.

And here's the beauty of it: if you practice enough, those doors will open. You'll learn to adapt, refine, and perfect your pitch in a way that feels authentic and effortless. You'll not only master the art of pitching, but you'll master the art of resilience.

The pure fact is that nobody becomes a master without practice. It's easy to assume that successful people were just born that way, but in reality, even those with talent have to work hard to maintain and improve. Like Jordan, they put in the hours behind the scenes when no one is watching.

You've taken aim. Now hit your target.

Practice doesn't make perfect. Practice makes progress and progress creates results.

Scan the QR Code and keep sharpening your skills inside the Pitch Secrets Resource Center (Chapter P).

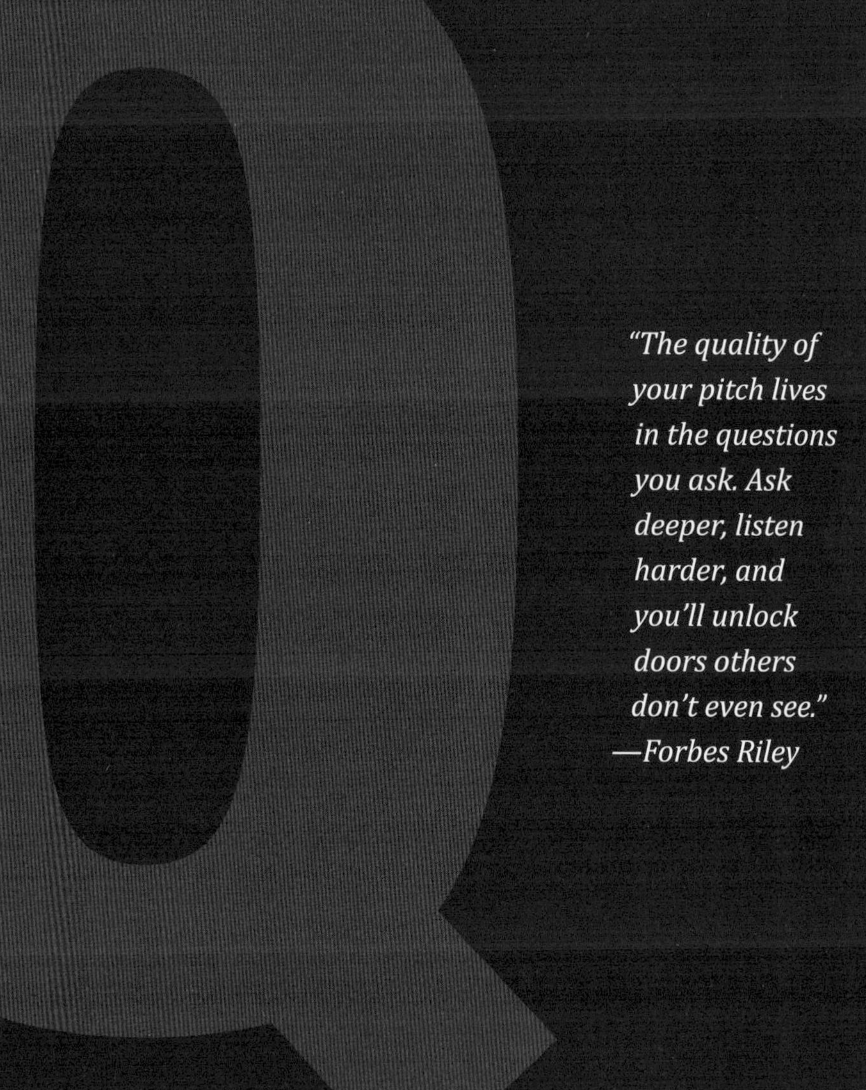

"The quality of your pitch lives in the questions you ask. Ask deeper, listen harder, and you'll unlock doors others don't even see."
—Forbes Riley

CHAPTER Q: Question

Question (noun): *A sentence worded or expressed so as to elicit information.*

The question you must ask yourself before pitching anything is: "What is the biggest problem my customer is suffering from?"

This shifts the focus from what you're selling to why they need it. When you identify this, you unlock the key to a powerful pitch because people don't buy products—they buy solutions.

I'm often told, "Forbes, you are such a great pitcher, you could sell ice to Eskimos!" But here is the truth: Eskimos don't suffer from a lack of ice. Pitching is not about convincing people to buy something they do not want, but instead, offering them a solution to a problem they have.

So, what would I pitch to Eskimos?

Firewood and blankets. Why? Because I understand their need for warmth and comfort, not more ice. A great pitch isn't about selling something just for the sake of selling; it's about deeply understanding the needs and desires of your audience. When you identify the real problem, you position yourself as a trusted provider of answers rather than someone pushing a product.

Think of a customer's struggle as the gap between where they are and where they want to be. It's the obstacle, challenge, or pain point preventing them from achieving their desired outcome.

A well-defined problem isn't generic; it's specific, relatable, and emotionally compelling.

For example:

- **Generic Problem:** "My customers want to lose weight."
- **Well-Defined Problem:** "My customers feel stuck because they've tried diets and workouts that didn't work, leaving them disappointed and unsure of what to do next."

The second example taps into emotions, frustration, confusion, and discouragement. These emotions are powerful because people don't just make decisions based on logic; they're driven by how they feel. Unlocking emotions and defining them allow you to drive home valuable pain points.

Introducing the Question Flip

Let's explore how to identify your customer's problem naturally in a conversation and use it to close. This is where the Question Flip comes in. This technique shifts the approach from telling to asking, guiding your audience to recognize their own challenges before you introduce the solution.

By asking the right questions, you guide them to recognize what they truly want in relation to your offer, naturally creating buy-in without resistance. People trust and commit to conclusions they reach on their own far more than those imposed upon them.

How the Question Flip Works

Let's start with our fitness trainer example. Most fitness coaches and weight loss programs dive straight into listing features, for example promoting a 90-day weight loss program or offering personal training services. However a more powerful approach is to set the stage with a question. This helps potential clients uncover their own motivation before you introduce your solution.

Step 1: Ask a Discovery Question

Your goal is to draw out the challenge rather than assuming it. This isn't just surface-level; it's about prompting real reflection.

Example: *"What's the biggest challenge you face when working to stay consistent with your fitness and weight loss goals?"*

Step 2: Let Them Acknowledge the Struggle

Instead of telling them what their problem is, let them say it themselves. When they voice their struggle, it becomes real and personal, not just something being sold to them.

Customer Response: *"I always feel overwhelmed in the gym and procrastinate too much about working out and eating healthy. I just have no willpower.*

Step 3: Flip the Question to Lead into Your Solution

Now, take their challenge and reframe it in a way that makes your program the obvious solution. This isn't a hard sell; it's a natural progression from their problem to your answer.

Response: *"If procrastination and overwhelm are holding you back, imagine how much easier it would be with a simple, step-by-step system that keeps you motivated and on track, with one-on-one accountability, without the struggle."*

Customer Response: *"Wow that would be amazing if someone helped me get through those tough times as I've never been effective on my own."*

The beauty of the Question Flip lies in its simplicity. When people articulate their own problems, they feel a sense of ownership over them. This self-awareness makes them more open to solutions, especially ones they feel they've discovered themselves.

Instead of facing resistance, you're met with curiosity and interest. The customer is no longer thinking, *Are they going to sell me something?* Instead, they're wondering, *Could this be the solution I've been looking for?*

Here is another example of selling a productivity app. Instead of launching into all the amazing features, you start with:

> **Discovery Question:** "What's the hardest part about staying organized at work?"
>
> **Customer Response:** "I struggle with keeping track of deadlines and managing my tasks efficiently."
>
> **Question Flip:** "If managing tasks is overwhelming, how much more productive do you think you'd be with an app that keeps everything organized in one place?"

Notice how natural that feels?

It doesn't sound like a pitch. It sounds like a conversation. By asking questions that make them reflect on their frustrations, fears, and desires, you're engaging both their hearts and minds.

After the initial Question Flip, don't stop there. Keep the conversation flowing with follow-up questions that deepen the connection:

- "How would it feel to finally have control over your schedule?"
- "What would it mean for your business if you could double your productivity?"
- "How would your life change if you consistently achieved your goals with less stress?"

These questions keep the focus on the customer's desired outcome, making your solution feel even more relevant.

The most powerful pitches don't feel like pitches. The Question Flip takes you from a salesy monologue to an engaging dialogue where the customer feels heard, understood, and ready to say "yes."

The Question Flip isn't just a strategy—it's the key to unlocking deeper connections and effortless persuasion. Instead of telling people what they need, you guide them to discover it for themselves. This shift removes resistance, builds trust, and makes your solution feel like the obvious next step.

The answers you're looking for are already there; you just need to look closer.

The right question brings clarity, builds trust, and makes your pitch feel like the natural next step. Stop guessing. Start uncovering what really matters.

Scan the QR Code to explore the Resource Center (Chapter Q) and sharpen your questioning skills.

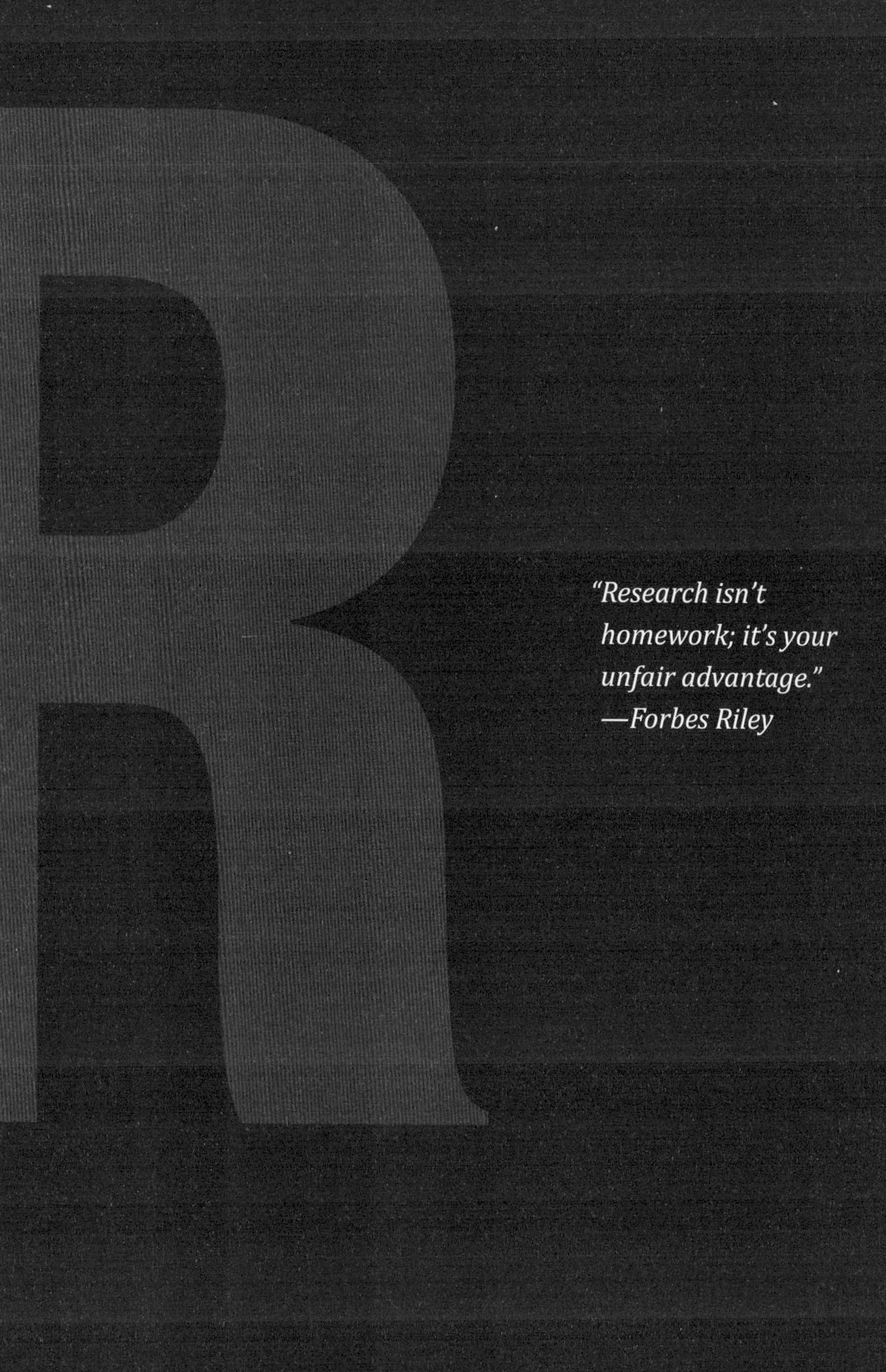

"Research isn't homework; it's your unfair advantage."
—Forbes Riley

CHAPTER R: Research

Research (noun): *The systematic investigation into and study of materials and sources in order to establish facts and reach new conclusions.*

What I'm about to share with you is one of my most powerful secrets to success as both a pitcher and a business owner. When we think of research, we often default to Googling or binge-watching YouTube tutorials, but there's a far more effective and insightful approach.

What if I told you there's a way to not only determine whether your offer is truly desirable, but also uncover how to stand out in the marketplace and ensure your offer thrives? Let me show you how.

It is important to understand and appreciate that you have competition—every industry does. Whether you're selling a product or service or have an idea, I guarantee you there's someone out there already offering something similar. But here's the game-changer: competition isn't the enemy; it's an opportunity.

Look at the great rivalries: Coke and Pepsi, Nike and Adidas, Burger King and McDonald's. Each brand has mastered its positioning, carved out a unique identity, and consistently improved by learning from the other. They don't just compete; they innovate.

One of the most valuable lessons I've learned is that to be the best, you must study the best. How? By buying from them. It might sound counterintuitive, but this approach has been pivotal in my journey.

When you invest in understanding what your competitors are doing well, you gain insights that can transform your own offer.

By purchasing from competitors, you get an insider's view of what attracts loyal customers and keeps them coming back. Is it the quality of the product? Their customer service? The unique branding?

By analyzing your competition, you can refine your own offerings, elevate your pitch, and gain an edge in your industry. It's not about copying; it's about learning and then outshining them with what you've discovered.

Let me tell you about the day research changed my life.

When I first discovered SpinGym, it was being sold as an office de-stressor, marketed as a simple tool for relieving tension at a desk. The product wasn't resonating, and the company was on the verge of shutting down. When I experienced it for the first time, something clicked. I didn't see an office toy. I could feel its potential as a serious fitness tool, especially for upper-body toning.

Having spent years in the fitness industry, including being inducted into the National Fitness Hall of Fame and selling over 1,500 fitness products, I instantly knew this was one of the most innovative upper-body devices I had ever encountered.

However, the owner didn't see it that way, insisting it was nothing more than a desk gadget. That night, I couldn't stop thinking about its potential, especially remembering my mom, who was 260 pounds and terrified to even step into a gym. I thought, *What if this could be the solution for people like her—simple, portable, and unintimidating?*

The next day, I approached the owner with a new vision. This product wasn't just a "toy." It had the potential to be a fitness tool that people could use at home, in the office, or on the go. It was compact yet powerful, designed to tone arms, back, and core by providing a full workout experience without the intimidation or pressure of stepping into a gym.

After persistent negotiations, I acquired the rights to the product and immediately began reimagining it. With my background in dance, pilates, and fitness certifications, I developed entirely new exercises and routines designed to target upper-body toning and created a fitness-focused identity for the product.

I innovated everything, from the branding and colors to how the SpinGym was positioned in the market. It wasn't just about having a great product; it was about solving a real problem in a way that resonated with people.

By listening to my audience, conducting hands-on research, and leveraging my expertise, I turned the SpinGym into a product that sold over 2 million units on HSN. This experience taught me that research isn't just about analyzing data; it's about uncovering the real wants and desires of your audience and presenting a solution that genuinely resonates.

My journey with SpinGym taught me that great ideas don't happen in ISOLATION. They emerge from deep research and a strong connection to the people you're serving. One of the most powerful ways to do that?

How You Gain Your Unfair Advantage

Step 1: Define Your Niche.

Get laser-focused on who you serve. A niche is simply a targeted segment of the market with specific needs. The tighter your niche, the easier it is to identify who your true competitors are.

Step 2: Select Your Competitors.

Choose 2–3 businesses offering similar solutions to your same audience. These will become your personal case studies.

Step 3: Analyze Their Offer. Start with the Basics.

- What exactly are they selling?
- How is your offer different or better?
- How are they priced and how do you compare?

Step 4: Dig Deeper. Study Their Positioning.

- What colors, visuals, and branding elements do they use to attract attention?
- What language, phrases, or emotional hooks do they lean on?
- How are they stacking value in their pitch?
- Which social media platforms are driving their engagement?

Step 5: Become Their Customer. Immerse Yourself.

- What upsells and downsells were presented during checkout?
- What email sequences did you receive after purchasing?
- How are they closing sales—online funnels, webinars, or direct calls?

Step 6: Observe the Post-Purchase Experience.

- How did they deliver the product?
- What bonuses, communities, or memberships were offered?
- Are you being retargeted with follow-up ads?
- What additional offers are they making once you're in their system?

By immersing yourself in your competitors' customer experience, you gain invaluable insights into their strengths, weaknesses, and strategies. This isn't about copying; it's about learning, innovating, and finding ways to offer something more unique and tailored to your audience's needs.

Innovation doesn't live in isolation.
It lives in observation.

Research taught me to see beyond the obvious, to empathize with the struggles of others, and to innovate in ways that truly mattered. For me, it started with my mom, but it grew into a mission to empower millions to feel strong, confident, and capable—all because I took the time to understand where the gap in the market was.

When you master the art of research, not just information-gathering, but true customer understanding, you position yourself to lead. You become the one who doesn't just offer something to buy, but offers something your customer feels was designed exactly for them.

The world doesn't reward the person who shouts the loudest. It rewards the one who listens the closest.

"Social media gives you a stage. Your pitch determines who stays to listen."
—Forbes Riley

CHAPTER S: Social Media

Social Media (noun): *Made up of websites, apps, and other platforms that allow users to share information and ideas with virtual communities through text, photos, videos, and more.*

Social media isn't just a tool; it's the lifeblood of modern communication. It's where your pitch finds its audience, your message creates impact, and your brand takes flight.

In the early stages of my TV host and acting career, the only way to get your message out to the masses was through gatekeepers—executive producers, PR agencies, and major advertisers. If you weren't invited to the table, you didn't get to play. But social media changed the game. Suddenly, anyone with a smartphone had a global stage. The barriers were torn down, and the power shifted from corporations to individuals. When I first started using social media, I underestimated its potential. I posted sporadically, treated it like a chore, and didn't realize that every post was an opportunity to connect, inspire, and influence. When I started treating my social media profiles like a business card, everything changed. I built relationships with clients, sold products, and even landed speaking engagements, all because of the impression my profile made.

And that is why YOU have more opportunities now than ever before. You don't need permission from a network, a big budget, or a PR team. You need strategy, authenticity, and engagement. But with endless voices competing for attention, how do you ensure that YOUR message stands out? How do you use social media to elevate your pitch, build credibility, and attract opportunities?

The most encouraging thing I can share with you is that you don't need a massive audience to see results. You just need the right audience. It's not about shouting your message to thousands; it's about speaking to those who really need to hear it.

How does this tie into pitching? It's all about communication. Your social media is an extension of your pitch, reflecting who you are and what you stand for. If your content is inconsistent with your brand or values, it can confuse your audience and weaken your message. Think of every post as an opportunity to communicate what you do in a way that excites, engages, and aligns with your audience. By showing up authentically and providing value, you're not just creating content. You're building trust, loyalty, and a foundation for a pitch that resonates. Social media becomes more than a platform; it's the stage for your story.

Whether it's Facebook, LinkedIn, Instagram, or TikTok, your profile tells the world who you are, what you stand for, and the value you bring. Think of it as your virtual business card, available 24/7, showcasing your personal brand, values, and expertise to potential clients, collaborators, and followers. When leveraged strategically, it can turn casual scrollers into loyal customers and valuable connections.

Let's get something clear: you do not need to be famous or become an influencer for your social media to have a positive effect on your business. The question is, how do you maximize your impact to create that positive effect? Let me share my "5 Social Media Secrets":

Social Media Secret #1: Secure Your Presence Everywhere

Think of your social media usernames like prime real estate. If you wait too long, someone else will claim your name, and reclaiming it later could be nearly impossible (or expensive!). Your first step is to establish a consistency across all platforms. Even if you're not ready to actively use every social media platform, claim your name NOW.

The must-have platforms are:

- ✓ Facebook
- ✓ Instagram
- ✓ LinkedIn
- ✓ TikTok
- ✓ YouTube
- ✓ X (Twitter)

You might be thinking, "Do I really need all of them?" **YES.**

Not because you need to post everywhere daily, but because visibility is credibility. In today's world, people will Google you before they trust you. If your name is missing or, worse, claimed by someone else, you lose instant authority.

Your brand must be future-proof. This is about control. Ownership. Presence.

You don't build influence by accident; you build it by design. When people search for you, they should find you.

Claim your space now. Post when you're ready. But own it today.

Social Media Secret #2: Build a Credible Profile

Your profile is your digital handshake, the first impression that speaks before you do. Prior to people engaging with your content, they quickly scan your profile picture, bio, and recent posts to decide if you're someone worth following. This moment of judgment happens in seconds, making it crucial that your profile works for you, not against you.

Each social platform has its own structure, from headers to bio space, and while they won't be identical, they should remain consistent, so that your audience recognizes you instantly. A strong, cohesive profile communicates who you are, what you stand for, and why people should pay attention.

- ✓ **Profile Picture:** A clear, professional, and friendly headshot—no blurry selfies, weird filters, or group photos.
- ✓ **Bio:** Who are you? What do you do? Why should they care? Keep it short, impactful, and value-driven.
- ✓ **Link:** Direct people to your website, offer, or a digital business card that guides them to your key resources.
- ✓ **Banner Image:** A professional, visually appealing banner that reinforces your brand or expertise.

Just remember, your profile isn't just about looking professional; it's about making an impact the moment someone lands on it.

Social Media Secret #3: Content is Your Currency

Content is how you establish authority, build trust, and turn casual followers into loyal fans. But it's not just about what you post; it's about how you present it and how it resonates.

Here's how to create content that works:

- **Educate with Value:** Share actionable tips, industry insights, and expert knowledge that your audience can apply immediately. Position yourself as a go-to resource.
- **Inspire Through Storytelling:** Use personal experiences, testimonials, and success stories to create an emotional connection. Show your audience what's possible for them.
- **Entertain and Be Relatable:** Infuse humor, behind-the-scenes moments, and raw authenticity to make your content engaging and memorable. People connect with real, not perfect.

- **Engage Like a Human:** Ask thought-provoking questions, encourage discussions, and respond to comments. Make your followers feel seen and heard.

- **Guide with a Clear Call to Action:** Every post should direct your audience toward the next step—whether it's following you, joining your community, downloading a free resource, or taking action on what they've learned.

The mistake I see over and over again is people confusing *posting* with *engaging*. Social media isn't about broadcasting. It's about starting conversations. The real growth happens not in how many posts you make, but in how many conversations you create. Every comment you leave, every direct message you respond to, every discussion you initiate builds relationship capital.

Social Media Secret #4: Engagement is the Ultimate Growth Hack

Each platform has its own personality and rules. LinkedIn isn't Facebook, and Instagram isn't TikTok. But they all share one common goal: to keep users engaged.

Think of it like hosting the best party in town. Your job isn't to sell to every guest; it's to create an environment where people want to stay, connect, and come back for more. When you do this right, the engagement happens naturally because people already know, like, and trust you.

Success on social media isn't about pushing out random content. It's about creating conversations that build relationships and amplify your reach. Here's how to make engagement your secret weapon:

- **Respond to DMs Like a Pro**—Stop treating your inbox like an afterthought! Reply with intention. Take the time to engage, build relationships, and add value instead of just dropping a generic response. Show people that you're not just a brand—you're a person they can trust and connect with. DMs aren't just messages; they're potential deals, partnerships, and game-changing opportunities waiting to happen.

- **Leave Thoughtful Comments**—Want to turn followers into superfans? Don't just drop emojis. Add value and make them feel seen! Ask them about their goals, respond with energy, and offer something meaningful—whether it's a quick tip, a helpful resource, or just a genuine interaction.

- **Join the Right Communities**—Success isn't just about what you know; it's about who knows YOU. If you want to grow your influence, get in the right rooms, both online and offline. That means being active in LinkedIn groups, Facebook communities, industry masterminds, and live discussions where the movers and shakers in your niche are already talking.

But here's the key:
Don't just sit back and watch

- **ENGAGE**. Ask questions, share insights, offer value, and make your presence known. The more you contribute, the more credibility and visibility you build. And trust me, when people see you consistently showing up and adding value, opportunities will come knocking.

Social Media Secret #5: Consistency is the Key to Trust

One of the biggest reasons people fail on social media is because they treat it like speed dating instead of a long-term relationship. They post sporadically, disappear for weeks, and wonder why their audience isn't growing.

Success comes from showing up consistently. Here's how to make it manageable:

- **Batch Your Content:** Set aside one day a week to create and schedule posts in advance. One day of work can produce a full week or month of consistent visibility.
- **Post at Peak Times:** Use platform insights to determine when your audience is most active.
- **Use Stories and Lives:** Instagram and Facebook Stories, as well as live videos, create real-time engagement and build deeper connections.

Social media rewards consistency and engagement. The more present you are, the more the algorithm favors your content.

Growing your social media presence can feel like an uphill battle at first. You're creating profiles, crafting posts, and reaching out to connect with people, often feeling like your efforts are going unnoticed. It's easy to question if all the hard work is worth it. But here's the secret: every post, every interaction, and every connection adds weight to your boulder, slowly pushing it closer to the tipping point.

Then, almost without realizing it, something incredible happens…the boulder starts to gain momentum on its own. People start engaging with your content, sharing your posts, and even recommending your page to others. This is when your presence shifts from struggling for attention to being a recognized voice in your niche. It's the magic of persistence paired with strategy, proving that social media success isn't about going viral overnight. It's about building momentum that carries you forward and keeps growing.

Social media is no longer optional; it's your open door to a global audience. But simply showing up isn't enough. Every post, every story, every comment is an opportunity to pitch—to stop the scroll, spark curiosity, and create trust.

The truth is, your audience is already waiting. They are scrolling. Searching. Listening. But they can't say yes to your offer if they can't find you.

So claim your space. Show up consistently. Speak your truth.

Because when you pitch with clarity, authenticity, and conviction, your followers don't just watch. They believe.

And when they believe, they buy.

Ready to optimize your social media presence and elevate your pitch?

If you're excited to rethink and rework your digital profiles, scan the QR Code to head over to the Resource Center (Chapter S), where I have free social media templates you can easily implement.

"Technology doesn't replace your pitch; it multiplies it."
—Forbes Riley

CHAPTER T: Technology

Technology (noun): *The application of scientific knowledge, tools, and techniques to create solutions, improve efficiency, and enhance human life.*

Technology is no longer optional. It's the driving force behind how we communicate, do business, and shape our future. It has shattered barriers, leveled the playing field, and given anyone with a smartphone access to knowledge, opportunity, and global audiences. But with all its power, it's also a double-edged sword. It can accelerate your success or leave you overwhelmed, distracted, and stagnant. The question isn't whether technology will change your life; it already has. The real question is: Are you using it to your advantage, or is it using you?

For entrepreneurs willing to embrace it, technology is the greatest tool for leverage. It allows you to automate tasks, reach millions, and scale businesses at speeds that were unimaginable just a decade ago. It enables personal brands to become industry leaders, with nothing more than a strong message and the ability to show up consistently. It puts the power of education, networking, and monetization in the hands of the individual, cutting out gatekeepers, and creating limitless possibilities. But for those who resist it, fear it, or fail to adapt, it becomes an anchor, holding them back while others surge ahead.

I learned this lesson the hard way.

It was during the COVID lockdown, and I was staring blankly at my computer screen, paralyzed. My business was floundering. I was watching my colleagues pivot to the digital world, launching online programs, building scalable systems, and thriving.

Meanwhile, I felt completely frozen. Ironically, I was helping others craft their digital pitches, writing video sales letters, and consulting on strategy—yet I couldn't seem to apply any of it to my own business.

Then my 17-year-old daughter, Makenna, walked into my office and changed everything.

"What are you doing, Mom?" she asked.

"Nothing," I replied, defeated. "I don't know what to do."

Without missing a beat, she said:

"Let me put you online. We can make a million dollars in a year."

I laughed. Until she showed me her six-figure bank account.

While I was stuck clinging to my comfort zone, my teenage daughter had quietly mastered backend technology. She was building systems for names like Joe Theismann and Les Brown, setting up automations, funnels, and entire online businesses while I was still debating how to even get started. Within 24 hours of launching my first webinar with her help, we made $25,000. That same funnel would eventually cross $1 Million in revenue, earning us the coveted 2 Comma Club Award.

That moment shattered my old story about technology. It wasn't my enemy. It wasn't my obstacle. It was my greatest ally, but only if I was willing to embrace it.

I've seen it happen firsthand. The entrepreneur with a brilliant product, but no online presence, wondering why no one is buying. The speaker with decades of experience who refuses to go live on social media, watching as younger, less experienced voices take the stage instead. The business owner clinging to outdated methods while their competitors leverage AI, automation, and digital platforms to work smarter, not harder.

Success isn't just about skill or experience anymore. It's about adaptability. Those who are willing to evolve with technology will thrive. Those who aren't will become obsolete.

Technology doesn't wait for anyone. Look at how it has transformed industries overnight. Streaming services replaced DVDs. Ride-sharing crushed taxis. Social media gave individuals more influence than major news networks. AI is now writing emails, creating marketing campaigns, and analyzing data at speeds no human can match. The businesses and brands that win are the ones that don't just keep up with change; they leverage it before everyone else does.

But let's be clear: technology is a tool, not a replacement. AI won't replace entrepreneurs, but entrepreneurs who use AI will replace those who don't. Automation won't eliminate human connection, but those who master it will have more time to focus on building relationships and scaling their impact. Digital platforms won't make traditional networking obsolete, but they will allow those who use them correctly to dominate their industries while others struggle to keep up.

This isn't about being tech-savvy; it's about being strategic. You don't need to master every new tool, jump on every new platform, or spend hours learning complex systems. You just need to ask yourself: What technology will help me move faster, work smarter, and expand my reach? The answer will be different for everyone, but the principle remains the same. Use technology as an amplifier, not a distraction.

This mindset shift changed everything for me: Technology isn't just a set of tools—it's your business partner. A partner that…

- Never sleeps
- Never takes vacation
- Works tirelessly to spread your message
- Multiplies your impact without multiplying your time

Some of the greatest opportunities today exist in the digital space, yet too many people hesitate because they don't fully understand it. They tell themselves they're "not good with tech," or "don't have time to learn new systems." But the truth is, technology is not complicated—staying stuck is.

If you've ever found yourself resisting technology, ask yourself why. Is it the fear of not knowing where to start? The overwhelm of too many options? The discomfort of stepping outside your routine? Whatever the reason, know this—technology isn't here to hold you back; it's here to set you free. It's the shortcut to reaching more people, automating the busywork, and unlocking the next level of your success. But only if you choose to embrace it.

Some will read this and continue doing things the way they always have. They'll keep waiting for the "right time" to learn new skills, set up their digital systems, or start showing up online. Others will recognize that technology is not the future; it's the present. They'll take action, experiment, and find ways to use it to their advantage. And those are the ones who will win.

Surviving the Tech Tsunami

As someone who grew up with the phone attached to a wall... I always feel like I'm playing catch-up. There's ALWAYS something new to learn, to figure out. Technology is supposed to make your life easier, but during that learning curve, it can feel like climbing Mount Everest in flip-flops.

Look, I get it. If you're feeling overwhelmed by technology, you're not alone. Every time I finally master an online tool, 3 new ones pop up. It's like playing whack-a-mole with software updates. But here's the truth bomb I had to swallow: in today's world, a great pitch alone isn't enough. You need technology to amplify your message, scale your impact, and yes—make those sales while you sleep.

I'm reminded of my dad... When email first appeared, he was 69 years old and he confidently declared, "This email nonsense will never last!" (Spoiler alert: it did.) The pace of change is dizzying. When he was young, technology evolved every 10–20 years. Now? It changes every 10–20 days. But here's the secret I learned the hard way: you don't have to master everything. You just need to embrace what moves the needle for your business.

Here's my proven strategy for handling tech overwhelm:

- **Set a Timer:** Spend 15–30 minutes daily getting familiar with new tools. Baby steps!
- **Batch Your Tech Problems:** Keep a running list and tackle them in groups—or better yet, ask for help.
- **Innovate Like a Turtle:** Small changes add up to big results.
- **Make Google Your BFF:** When in doubt, search it out!
- **Avoid the Scroll Spiral:** Learning online is great, until it turns into a time warp. Stay intentional.

So, where do YOU stand? Are you letting technology intimidate you, or are you ready to harness it, master it, and use it to accelerate your success? Because in this fast-moving world, the biggest risk isn't using new technology; it's getting left behind by those who do.

Here are some of my tried-and-true Digital Pitch favorites:

1. **CRM Systems** (*Your "Pitch Memory"*)
   A good CRM is like a personal assistant with a photographic memory. It tracks every interaction and follow-up, ensuring no prospect slips through the cracks.
2. **Otter** (*Your "Pitch Perfecter"*)
   Record your pitch, and it instantly transcribes it into text. Spot filler words, tighten sections, and refine your delivery—it's like a 24/7 pitch coach.
3. **Canva** (*Your "Pitch Designer"*)
   Create stunning visuals in minutes. Forget struggling with PowerPoint and Photoshop, Canva puts a design team in your pocket and is evolving with AI.
4. **Cloud Tools** *(Your "Collaboration Hub")*
   Google Docs and Dropbox enable seamless collaboration, letting teams work together anytime, anywhere.

5. **GSD** *(Your "Business-in-a-Box")*
   This all-in-one platform simplifies funnel-building, email marketing, and more. It's perfect for streamlining your digital business.

6. **AI** *(Your "Unlimited Advantage")*
   This fast-growing technology is designed to increase productivity, expand your creativity, and level up your growth. It does, however, come with a warning. Every day, there seems to be a new AI popping up. So my thought to you is catch up to keep up.

Each of these tools plays a powerful role in my multi-8-figure online empire—that's exactly why I recommend them to you. But let me give it to you straight: start small. Pick the one tool that solves your biggest pitching headache. Master it. Own it. Then stack on the next. That's how real momentum is built.

The future of pitching isn't either/or—it's both/and.

Your authentic voice + the reach of technology = unstoppable impact

That sweet spot is where pitching becomes effortless, scalable, and deeply impactful. It's where your story connects with the right audience at the right time, without you having to be in the room.

It's where magic meets momentum.

Look, I still LOVE face-to-face pitching. There's nothing like the electric energy of a live room. But now? My message works while I sleep. My pitches close sales while I'm on vacation. And yes, that webinar my daughter and I created, *Pitch Secrets MasterClass*, is still generating sales around the clock.

Here's the golden rule: technology should serve your pitch, never complicate it. Choose tools that feel natural, amplify your strengths, and get results. Your pitch might be personal, but your impact?

Global. Limitless. Unstoppable.

The technology train is leaving the station. You can either watch it go by, like my father did with email, or hop aboard and enjoy the ride.

Scan the QR Code to visit the Resource Center (Chapter T) and explore my top recommended AI tools and the latest digital innovations. *Full steam ahead!*

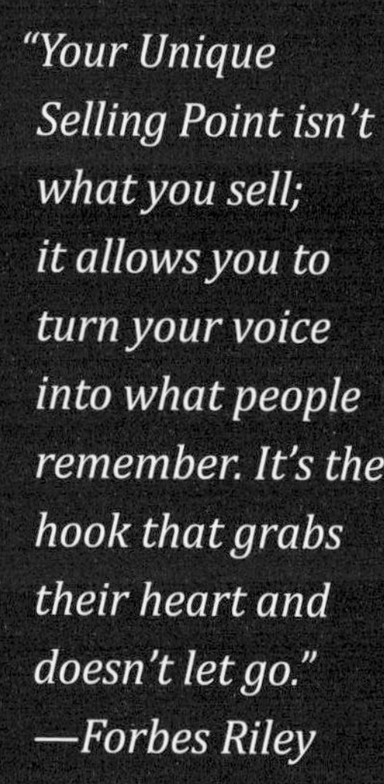

"Your Unique Selling Point isn't what you sell; it allows you to turn your voice into what people remember. It's the hook that grabs their heart and doesn't let go."

—Forbes Riley

CHAPTER U: Unique Selling Point (USP)

Unique Selling Point (USP) (noun): *A concise statement that explains why a business or product is better than its competitors.*

It's 2:00 a.m., and I'm standing under blazing lights on a live TV set, pitching to millions of people who can change the channel with one click of their remote. I had just seconds to grab their attention and convince them that what I'm holding is worth their time. That's where a Unique Selling Point comes in. A USP is the one thing that sets your product, service, or idea apart. It's the reason someone chooses you over the competition.

At the time I was selling my fitness innovation, SpinGym, a sleek, compact tool that at first glance looked like a simple toy. But once you felt the burn, once you experienced the power packed into this device, you were hooked. The challenge? I couldn't just tell people it was effective; I had to prove it without them ever experiencing it.

Saying it provided up to 24 pounds of resistance and was a great arm workout was accurate, but not compelling. Why would someone toss out their $10 resistance band and invest $40 in my product that, on the surface, seemed to do the same thing? That's where USP, Unique Selling Point, came into play.

I had to highlight what made SpinGym different, better, and absolutely essential. First, versatility. Unlike resistance bands that could snap, lose tension over time, or require multiple bands for different levels of resistance, SpinGym offered an all-in-one solution. Its unique design adapted to your movements, providing a dynamic and controlled workout for every fitness level—anytime, anywhere. That was my first USP: A one-size-fits-all fitness solution, replacing bulky equipment and resistance bands with a compact, adaptable workout.

Next, I emphasized portability. Sure, a resistance band can fit in a bag, but can you use it in your car while waiting to pick up the kids? At your desk between meetings? Sitting at a café, waiting for a friend? No! But SpinGym made it possible. It wasn't just a fitness tool; it was a lifestyle upgrade. That was my second USP: A compact, on-the-go fitness solution that fits in your pocket.

Combining these 2 USPs allowed me to naturally showcase the product's advantages, making it clear why this was the superior solution. But I didn't stop there. I always anchor my USP to a personal story, something real that explains why this feature matters to me. What experience shaped my belief in this product? What moment made me realize its true value? By sharing that emotional connection, I wasn't just selling a product. I was inviting my audience to see why it mattered to them, too.

The result? The phones lit up, and SpinGym sold out in record time.

This is the heart of a powerful USP. It's not just about what makes your product different from the competition; it's about why that difference matters to you as the pitcher. Your USP should be:

1. **Unique:** It differentiates you from the competition.
2. **Relevant:** It connects with your audience's needs, desires, or problems.
3. **Clear:** It communicates the value or benefit in a simple, understandable way.

The SpinGym's USP wasn't just about its features; it was about the promise it delivered: fitness that fits into your life, wherever you are. Combine that promise with a compelling story, and you have the magic formula for a winning pitch.

Your USP isn't just a tagline or marketing message; it's the foundation of your brand and the soul of your pitch. It's what helps you cut through the noise, attract attention, and build loyalty by delivering something your audience can't get anywhere else.

Another great example is McDonald's and Burger King. They both sell burgers and fries, but their USPs couldn't be more different. McDonald's built its brand around consistency, speed, and family-friendly experiences, ensuring that no matter where you are in the world, a Big Mac tastes the same. Burger King, on the other hand, positioned itself as the flame-grilled alternative, emphasizing customization with its famous "Have It Your Way" slogan. While both brands dominate the fast-food industry, their USPs cater to different customer preferences.

Finding your USP isn't just about listing features; it's about understanding what makes your offer different, better, and more valuable than anything else on the market. Follow these steps to uncover and craft a compelling USP that resonates with your audience.

Step 1: Identify Your Features

- ❑ List out every feature and benefit of your product or service.

Understanding your unique value begins with a detailed breakdown of what you provide. Explore every function, advantage, and distinguishing detail. Even minor elements can contribute to an offer that stands out.

Step 2: Compare with Competitors

- ❑ Find 3 competitors with similar products or services.
- ❑ Write down their features and list yours against theirs.
- ❑ Pinpoint where your product excels, stands out, or provides enhanced value.

Your competitors have similar offers, but your edge comes from what you do better. Look for what you've added, improved, or solved that they haven't. Maybe it's a better design, faster results, more convenient, or a more personalized experience. These elements define your competitive edge.

Step 3: Define Your USP

- ❑ Highlight the key differences that make you stand out.
- ❑ Transform these standout qualities into a concise, persuasive statement.

Your USP isn't just about what your product does; it's about why someone should choose you over the competition. Focus on how your unique features solve a specific problem in a way no one else does.

Step 4: Tie It to a Personal Story

- ❑ Ask yourself: Why does this matter to you?
- ❑ What personal experience inspired you to sell or affiliate with that particular product or service?
- ❑ How can you emotionally connect your USP to your audience?

Every strong USP has a story behind it. Think about what inspired you to create this solution. Was it a personal struggle? A frustration with existing options? A moment of realization? When you attach an emotional reason behind your USP, it resonates deeper with your audience.

Step 5: Integrate It into Your Pitch

- ❑ Make it clear how your product transforms your audience's life.

Your USP forms the cornerstone of your message, driving every pitch and marketing effort. It's not just a feature—it's the story, the solution, and the reason why your audience feels compelled to choose you. Show them how your offering changes their life in meaningful ways and why it's the obvious, undeniable choice.

In your pitch, your USP isn't just a talking point; it's the anchor that holds your entire message together. It's not about pushing a product; it's about weaving a story and delivering a solution that resonates on a deeper level.

In a world overflowing with options, your USP is what sets you apart. It's not about being the loudest voice in the room; it's about being the one people can't ignore. When you craft a clear, compelling USP, you don't just compete—you dominate.

So take the time to refine it, test it, and let it shape every aspect of your pitch. Because when your USP is solid, your pitch doesn't just inform; it inspires, influences, and transforms.

Your USP is your lightbulb moment, the spark that makes people stop, pay attention, and say *"That's exactly what I need."*

Scan the QR Code to access the Resource Center (Chapter U) and download your USP checklist.

It's time to illuminate what makes you unforgettable.

V

"The play button is the most compelling call-to-action on the internet."

—Michael Litt

CHAPTER V: Video

Video (noun): *A sequence of moving images, often accompanied by sound, used to convey information, tell a story, or entertain.*

Have you ever wished that after delivering a perfect pitch and closing multiple deals, you could just hit replay and have it work for you over and over again? That's exactly what video allows you to do—it lets your best pitch keep selling for you, 24/7. But here's the catch: if your video doesn't look professional, sound clear, or capture attention immediately, your message gets lost before it even has a chance to land.

I love video, and as you know, I've built my career in front of the camera, from TV and movies to infomercials and live home shopping. One thing I've learned along the way is that how you present yourself on video is just as important as what you're saying. When pitching on camera, being comfortable and natural is essential, but that's just the start. Since your audience can't touch or experience the product firsthand, you have to bridge the gap by making them feel the solution.

Today's world revolves around video. From YouTube and TikTok to Facebook Lives, Instagram Stories, and Zoom calls, video has become the dominant way we connect and communicate. What once required a Hollywood budget now sits in the palm of your hand.

As someone who has spent decades in front of the camera, whether on TV, in movies, or hosting infomercials, I've watched video evolve from a luxury into an absolute necessity. Research confirms that when given the choice between video and text, 72% of people choose video. Why? Because video isn't just seen—it's felt. It taps into visual and auditory senses, making your pitch more than just words on a page; it becomes an experience.

When it comes to pitching on camera, there are key elements you must implement to ensure your message is clear, compelling, and effective:

✓ Talk to One Person

The camera lens might feel like a black hole at first, but here's the secret: you're not addressing a faceless crowd; you're talking to *one person*. Suddenly, that intimidating camera lens becomes a bridge to a real conversation.

Imagine your best friend, your dream client, or that one person who needs your message today. Speak to them like it's just the two of you. When you make your audience feel like you're having a heartfelt conversation instead of delivering a generic speech, you create a bond that builds connection, trust, and impact. This simple shift transforms your energy and authenticity to a look of confidence.

✓ Stop the Fidget Fest

The camera catches *everything*, so let's keep those nervous habits in check! No swaying, no rocking, and definitely no twiddling your fingers like you're solving a Rubik's Cube. Own your space with calm, purposeful movements that radiate confidence. When you're in control, your message shines brighter and your audience feels your energy, not your jitters!

✓ Master Your Tone, Pacing, and Passion

Your voice is your superpower, so use it! Don't rush like you're hosting an auction or slow it down to bedtime-story mode. Find that sweet spot! Think of your voice as a roller coaster: a little up, a little down, and just enough excitement to keep the ride unforgettable.

And let's be real: if you're not pumped about what you're pitching, why should the listener be? Passion isn't just heard; it's felt. When you show how much you care, your audience will believe in your message and feel like they can't live without it. Enthusiasm is contagious, so let it shine!

✓ Frame Yourself Well

How you show up on camera speaks volumes! Set yourself up for success by keeping it simple: make sure the camera is at eye level so it feels like you're looking right at them. A clean, uncluttered background says you're focused and professional. Finally, good lighting is essential. Investing in a ring light or softbox can make all the difference in creating a polished, engaging presence.

When you feel good about how you look, you'll shine with confidence, and trust me, your audience will feel it too!

✓ Sound Like a Pro

If they can't hear you clearly, they'll stop listening. No one has time to strain through muffled audio or background distractions to understand what you are saying. A quality microphone isn't just a "nice-to-have," it's essential for your voice to be clearly heard. That paired with a quiet space, not a barking dog or the lawn mower outside, makes all the difference.

Crisp, clear sound doesn't just elevate your audio; it elevates *you*, making your message more powerful and your presence more professional. Trust me, your voice deserves to be heard—loud, clear, and confident!

✓ Keep It Short, Sweet, and Send Them Somewhere

Attention spans today are shorter than a TikTok dance, so hook your audience fast, get to the point, and make every second count. No rambling allowed! Once you've captured their interest, don't leave them wondering what's next. End with a clear, confident call to action that guides them exactly where you want them to go. Whether it's clicking a link, scheduling a call, or making a purchase, be bold, be direct, and leave no room for hesitation. You're in the driver's seat, so steer them toward an unforgettable finale!

When it comes to pitching on camera, it's not about being perfect; it's about being real. The camera isn't your obstacle—it's your opportunity. Speak with purpose, focus on the one person who needs you, and let your passion lead the way.

It's not about perfection; it's about presenting yourself in a way that reflects your confidence and professionalism. Lighting, angles, wardrobe, and even how you carry yourself can make a huge difference in how you come across.

If you've ever doubted your ability to be on camera, it's time to flip the script. The world needs your voice, your perspective, your truth. Don't let fear hold you back. Instead, see every video as a chance to leave a mark, to inspire someone in a way only you can.

Scan the QR Code to check out Chapter V in our Free Resource Center.

Lights, camera... it's time to take ACTION!

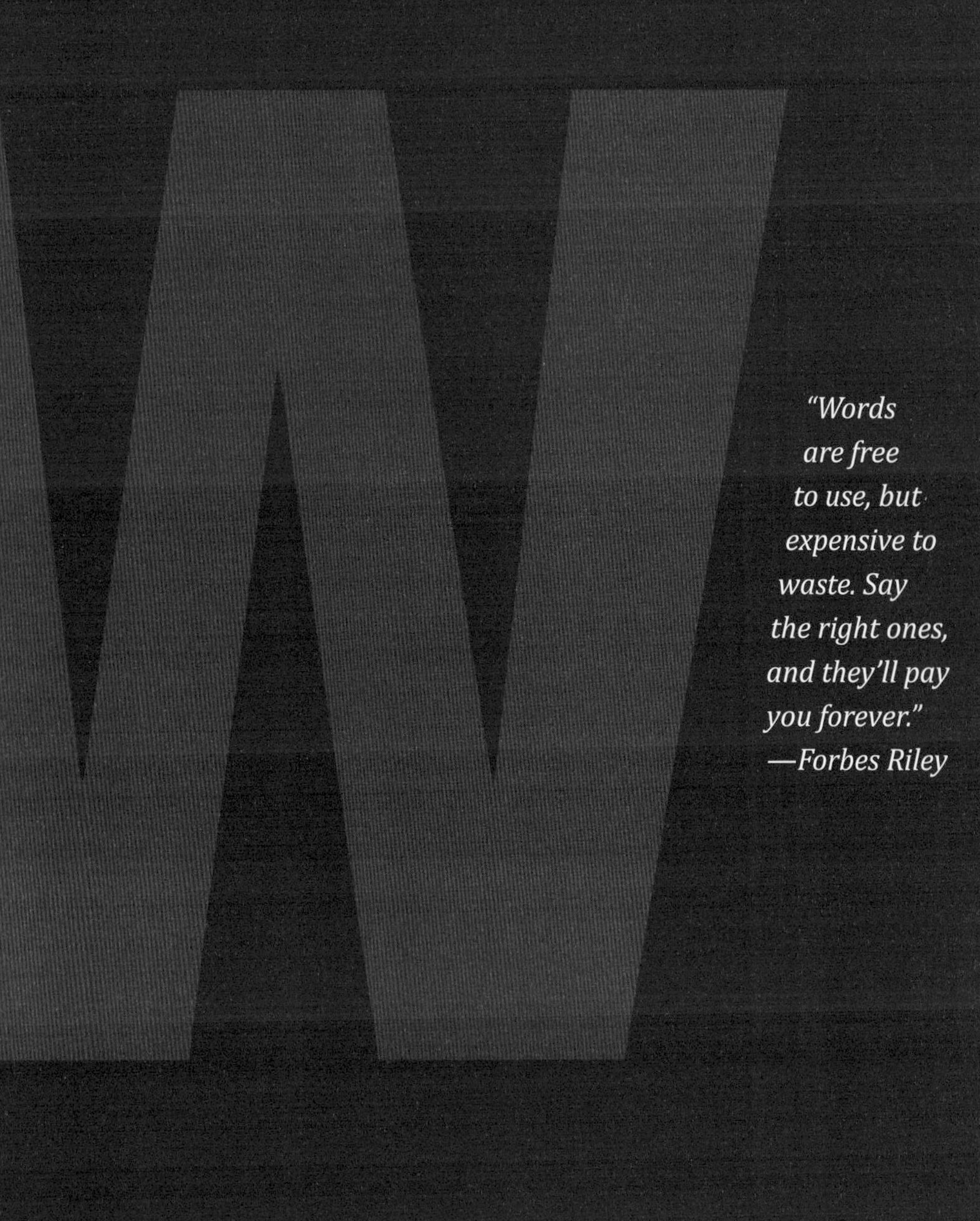

"Words are free to use, but expensive to waste. Say the right ones, and they'll pay you forever."

—Forbes Riley

CHAPTER W: Words

Words (noun): *Units of language that convey meaning, consisting of one or more spoken sounds or written symbols, used to communicate ideas, emotions, or actions.*

One word can change everything. I learned this lesson early in my career when pitching fitness products on TV. During one live show, I kept saying "This *could* help you get fit." My producer pulled me aside and said, "Forbes, stop saying 'could.' Say 'will.' Watch what happens." That simple change, from "could" to "will," doubled our sales in the next hour. One word made the difference between viewers sitting on their couch versus reaching for their phones to buy.

Words are everything in the world of pitching. They're the foundation of how we connect, influence, and persuade others to see our vision, buy into our ideas, or invest in our solutions. Think about it: every time you open your mouth to pitch, the words you choose either build trust or break it. They either pull your audience in or push them away.

To master this skill, you must be intentional about what you say, how you say it, and just as importantly, what you avoid saying. The right language paints a vivid picture, allowing your audience to envision themselves experiencing the transformation of your product or service. When done correctly, your words don't just inform—they inspire action and drive the sale.

Let me share something that changed my entire approach to pitching that I drill into all my students, clients, and even co-hosts on shows: I call these the "7 Deadly Phrases." These expressions can kill your pitch faster than they can say "Let me think about it." Every time one of these slips into your presentation, it's like putting a tiny crack in your audience's confidence.

The "7 Deadly Phrases" That Kill Your Pitch

1. **"Actually..."**

   Sounds harmless? It's not. When you use this word, it comes across as defensive or uncertain, as if what you are saying is not the truth. It can make you appear surprised, immediately taking down your credibility.

   For Example: "I, actually, closed 3 sales today" versus definitely stating "I closed 3 sales today." Why would you undermine a fact?

2. **"Basically..."**

   Much like the word "actually," this filler word subtly weakens your message and creates unnecessary doubt. Saying, "Basically, I graduated with a PhD" or "Basically, I teach women how to feel empowered" immediately makes your statement sound less certain, as if you're downplaying your own expertise. The question is, do you or don't you? Why sabotage the credibility of what you're saying?

   Many people use words like this in an attempt to sound humble, but in reality, it only serves to dilute their authority. Own your expertise and speak with confidence. There's no need to soften the impact of your accomplishments.

3. **"Like..."**

   The moment this filler creeps in, your professionalism walks out. It's one of the biggest culprits of weak communication, slipping into sentences and diluting your message. Overuse of "like" makes you sound unprepared, creating the impression that you're grasping for words rather than delivering a strong, confident pitch.

   Every unnecessary "like" chips away at your credibility and weakens your impact. For example, saying, "I'm, like, confident this product will help," doesn't convey as much conviction as simply saying, "I'm confident this product will help."

4. **"You know..."**

   No, they don't know. That's why they're listening to you. Another filler phrase that adds zero value to your pitch. When you say, "you know," it assumes the audience already understands something, which could make your point seem redundant and disconnect you from your listeners.

   This phrase is so overused that it makes it seem like you're seeking reassurance rather than delivering a confident statement.

5. **"Um..."**

   It's the tiny crack that can weaken the foundation of trust. Every time you say it, you're unconsciously signaling hesitation, and your audience feels it. Instead of letting filler words like "um" sneak in while you search for the right words, harness the power of the pause. Silence isn't awkward; it's commanding.

   A well-placed pause radiates confidence and authority, drawing your audience in rather than pushing them away. So, ditch the "um" and own the moment!

6. **"Try/Trying..."**

   These words are sneaky little traps. As my mentor once said, "Yoda nailed it—there is no try." Saying you're "trying" is like planting a seed of doubt. It hints that you've already failed or that you're not fully committed. And guess what? In pitching, that's deadly. Own the failure if it happens, grab the lesson, and move forward. But don't hide behind "trying." Speak with confidence, take action, and make things happen. There's no power in trying, only in doing.

7. **"I don't know..."**

   Three words that can slam the door on possibility. Instead of admitting uncertainty, pivot with power. Say, "That's a great question. Let me get back to you with the best answer." Or

"Let me find out for you." It's a simple shift that keeps you in control, both in pitching and in life. And here's the thing: When you stop relying on "I don't know," you'll be amazed to discover how often you *do* know. It's all about keeping the doors of opportunity wide open and owning your ability to figure things out.

WARNING: These phrases aren't just harmless fillers—they're trust killers.

Each one chips away at your authority and weakens your message. Every time you let one of these phrases slip into your pitch, you're diminishing your message and losing a bit of the audience's trust. But here's the good news: once you eliminate these 7 phrases, you create space for power words that transform your pitch. Here's what to use instead:

"Imagine"—Activates dreams and paints a vivid picture.

"Transform"—Promises meaningful, positive change.

"Exclusive"—Sparks desire and urgency.

"Discover"—Invites curiosity and exploration.

"Experience"—Makes it personal and tangible.

Here's how this works in real life:

Instead of saying, "I'm actually trying to show you how this product could basically help..."

Say: "Let me show you how this product will transform your experience."

Feel the difference? The second version isn't just more confident; it's more compelling. It makes people lean in and want to know more.

But words alone aren't enough. Your tone and body language need to match your message. I once watched a pitcher destroy a million-dollar opportunity by delivering powerful words with weak energy. Stand tall, make eye contact, and let your passion fuel your words. Your audience isn't just listening to what you say; they're feeling how you say it.

Mastering your words means mastering your influence. Every pitch, every conversation, and every opportunity is shaped by the language you choose.

The best communicators aren't just great talkers: they're precise, intentional, and unforgettable. Less fluff, more power. Less hesitation, more confidence.

Words aren't just what you say. They are what you sell. Every pitch rises or falls before the offer ever leaves your lips. People don't buy your product first; they buy your confidence, your certainty, your conviction.

Own your words, and you control the outcome. Because in the end, it's never about having the best product. It's about having the most powerful pitch.

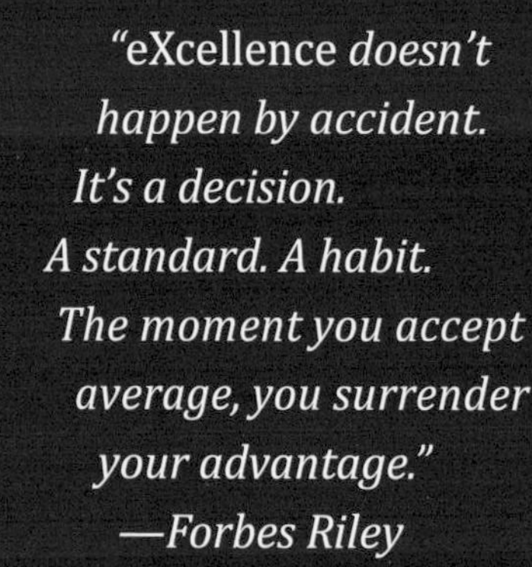

"eXcellence *doesn't happen by accident. It's a decision. A standard. A habit. The moment you accept average, you surrender your advantage."*

—Forbes Riley

CHAPTER X: eXcellence

eXcellence (noun): *The relentless commitment to rise above average, to deliver superior results, and to continuously raise the standard in everything you do. eXcellence isn't a single act—it's a habit, a mindset, and the secret advantage that separates good from unforgettable.*

eXcellence isn't just a word; it's a standard, a mindset, and the secret ingredient to a pitch that captivates and converts. And yes, I know it technically starts with an "e," but let's be real: X-ray and xylophone don't fit in our A to Z journey of pitching. So, for the sake of mastering your message, let's redefine "X" in this chapter as the pursuit of eXcellence.

While mediocrity whispers "good enough," eXcellence demands "exceptional." It's present in every aspect of your pitch, from your preparation to your delivery, from your first word to your closing statement.

eXcellence isn't just an aspiration; it's about the relentless pursuit of improvement. Think of it as your pitch's DNA. It shows in the way you:

- Research your audience until you understand their needs better than they do.
- Craft your message with the precision of a master jeweler.
- Deliver your pitch with the confidence of someone who has done their homework.
- Adapt and improve based on every experience, whether success or failure.

When you commit to eXcellence, you're not just checking boxes; you're creating an experience that resonates long after you've left the room. It's about setting a standard so high that even your "off days" outshine others' best efforts.

A common mistake many make is confusing eXcellence with perfection. The truth is, *perfection is a myth that paralyzes progress, while eXcellence is a mindset that fuels growth.*

eXcellence says: "Keep improving."
Perfection says: "You're not good enough."

Perfection stops you in your tracks, but eXcellence moves you forward. Your goal is not to be flawless; it's to continuously refine, learn, and evolve as a masterful pitcher. **Don't let the perfect ruin the good.**

Perfection held me back for years. It kept me from speaking, from sharing my message, and, believe it or not, from publishing my books. I had 6 almost finished books sitting on my computer, unpublished, because they weren't *perfect enough*. Maybe I needed more edits, maybe more research, maybe just... something more.

Then one day, I had a wake-up call.

First, someone believed in me and really saw what I had to offer and gave me that push. And second, I had to take my own advice.

I was coaching so many people, watching them break through their limiting beliefs, publishing their books and yet here I was, sitting on a gold mine of knowledge, afraid to release it. I finally said to myself:

"Forbes, if you don't share what you know and you take all this with you to the grave... shame on you."

That hit hard. Because the truth is, I've built a career, made millions, and changed lives by teaching people to pitch, but if I never documented it, never put it in a book, never left a blueprint, what kind of legacy would I leave? My daughter, Makenna, made me realize that if I really wanted to create something lasting, I had to stop waiting for perfection and just get my eXcellent work out there.

And that's why this book exists.

But here's the irony: people have always loved my writing. I wasn't a procrastinator. I was afraid of judgment. The world didn't need my perfection. They needed my experience. My version. My truth.

Your Message Deserves to Be Heard

So if you're sitting on an idea, a book, a product, a training, a course and you haven't released it because you're waiting for it to be perfect... shame on you.

Take a step back and ask yourself:

- ❑ If this never gets out into the world, will people be missing something valuable?
- ❑ Am I the only one who can teach it this way?
- ❑ What opportunities, lives, or businesses might never be changed if I stay silent?

For me, the answer was clear. Nobody on the planet teaches pitching the way I do. No one has my history, my background, my success. And if I stayed silent, if I only thought about it but never took action, then one day I'd die, and everything I've learned over my lifetime would disappear with me. That's why I write. That's why I teach. That's why I create videos and live trainings... because if I don't, who will?

So let me be blunt: You can't help anyone if you don't get your message out there. Stop waiting. Stop hesitating. The world needs your version of what only you can offer.

And remember: Perfection is what stops you. eXcellence is what moves you forward.

Perfection paralyzes. eXcellence propels.

If you want to make an impact, you have to take action—consistently.

It's not about being flawless. It's about raising your standards and showing up every day like it matters. Because it does.

eXcellence isn't a one-time act—it's a habit in motion.

As Jack LaLanne always said, "It's not what you do some of the time, it's what you do all the time that matters."

Scan the QR Code to access the Resource Center (Chapter X) and download your eXcellence Checklist.

Make exceptional your standard.

Y

"You are the
sum of the
obstacles
you overcome."
—Forbes Riley

CHAPTER Y: You

You (noun): *A beautiful, wonderful, loved person who is usually intelligent and occasionally thoughtful, and who is often misunderstood.*

There's a reason some people captivate an audience, close million-dollar deals, and effortlessly command a room while others struggle to get a single "yes." It's not just the words they say or the strategy they use—it's them. It's their presence, their confidence, and their belief in what they're saying.

And yet, most people don't realize that the obstacles standing in their way aren't external—they're internal. The greatest barriers you will ever face are the ones you don't even realize exist: the stories you've been telling yourself, the fears you've carried for years, and the subconscious decisions you made as a child that still dictate how you show up today.

Your confidence, passion, and commitment are what make you stand out. You are the secret sauce that makes everything else work, which is why *Pitch Secrets A to Z* began with you and your attitude, and now we're coming full circle.

You don't see things in life as they are; you see them as YOU are. This is one of the most powerful truths I've learned in my decades of pitching and teaching others to pitch. The more awareness you have of yourself, and the more you embrace who you are, the more the world shifts in response. If you've read the chapters B for Belief and F for Forbes It, you now understand how important it is to have unwavering faith in yourself and that you shape your reality.

Let me share something deeply personal. Through my work, I've come to understand that our most powerful limitations often trace back to decisions we made as young children, around 4 or 5 years old, when we were just beginning to make sense of the world.

It's easy to see how major events like the loss of a loved one, a traumatic accident, or abuse could shape our lives in profound ways. But what about the smaller, seemingly insignificant moments?

A harsh word from a teacher, an embarrassing experience at school, or a parent dismissing your ideas—these can also plant seeds that, over time, grow into patterns of procrastination, self-sabotage, or fear of stepping into your full potential.

A powerful example of this is a student of mine, a highly successful CEO, who was on the verge of being fired because despite her qualifications, she couldn't conduct board meetings or pitch investors—an essential part of her role. Every time she went to speak in front of others, she got so nervous and upset that she would throw up, her hands would get clammy, and she would just freeze. Despite being highly qualified, this one challenge was going to end her career.

After exhausting every option, from various coaches to therapists, nothing worked. Frustrated and out of answers, she came to me as her last hope, desperate to learn how to present on stage in a way that felt natural and effortless. What she didn't realize was that her fear wasn't just about public speaking—it was rooted in something much deeper.

Many people don't know this about me but my expertise stretches far beyond pitching and business strategy. In my 20s I became obsessed with neuroscience, NLP, and how the brain works, all in an effort to overcome my own blocks.

That journey of education and becoming a certified practitioner led me to developing a process of eliminating fear and limiting beliefs unlike anything else on this planet. I know that's a bold statement, but after working with thousands of people, I can confidently say, this process works.

So when she told me about her problem, I knew it went beyond just the fear of being on stage. I took her through my process, and what we uncovered changed everything. It turned out that when she was 7 years old, she had an embarrassing experience while giving a show-and-tell presentation in class. Overcome with nerves, she peed on herself in front of her classmates. They laughed, the teacher failed to step in, and in that moment, she made a subconscious decision: Never speak in public again.

Though she had long forgotten the incident, the decision she made as a child stayed with her, silently dictating her adult fears. Every time she stepped up to speak, her body reacted as if she were that little girl all over again. By identifying and addressing the underlying cause, I took her through my reframing process of BREAKthru, isolating the root cause, and rewiring her belief system. The transformation was immediate.

Not only did she keep her position as CEO, but she went on to write a book on success in the corporate world and delivered a flawless TEDx Talk. The fear that once controlled her was gone, replaced by confidence and clarity.

I invite you to take a moment and reflect about your fears or limiting beliefs when it comes to pitching, speaking, or simply turning your goals into reality. In my years of coaching people around the world, I've discovered one universal truth: the only thing standing between where you are now and where you want to be is...

YOU.

- **YOU** have the power to become a dynamic, confident speaker.
- **YOU** have the power to build a thriving, successful business.
- **YOU** have the power to achieve financial freedom.

But if that nagging little voice keeps whispering, *"You're not enough,"* or *"You're not ready,"* I can tell you with absolute certainty, the issue isn't coming from your present. You're holding onto something from your past.

As I explained in Chapter M for Mindset, the beliefs we hold about ourselves don't just appear out of nowhere. They are shaped by our earliest experiences, often rooted in moments we don't even consciously remember. And yet, those old fears, limiting beliefs, and subconscious decisions continue to steer our actions today.

That's why you'll hear me say, "Stop letting your 4-year-old drive the bus."

What does that mean? It means there's a moment from your childhood, just like the story of the CEO I shared above, that's still controlling your thoughts, behaviors, and confidence today. Maybe it was a time you were bullied, rejected, or abused. In that moment, you made a decision about yourself, about life, and about what's possible for you. And whether you realize it or not, that decision is still running in the background, shaping the way you show up in your career, your relationships, and your ability to take bold action.

For some, those childhood decisions serve them, but for many, they don't. The good news? You have the power to rewrite the story.

That hesitation, that lingering voice of doubt, it's not coming from who you are today; it's coming from an old story, a decision made years ago that's still running your life. And until you break through that subconscious block, no amount of strategy, training, or motivation will truly set you free.

That's exactly why I created *BREAKthru with Forbes Riley,* a transformational experience designed to help you uncover the hidden barriers holding you back, shatter your limiting beliefs, and step fully into your power.

Over the past 35 years, I've helped thousands of people achieve success, not just in their businesses, but in every area of their lives. From high-level executives to struggling entrepreneurs, I've guided people just like you to overcome the fears, doubts, and self-sabotaging patterns that have kept them stuck.

If you're curious to explore how your life can more easily fit together, I invite you to scan the QR Code to access the Resource Center (Chapter Y) and find information on how you can BREAKthru.

Your past doesn't define your future, unless you let it.

"Zoom isn't just a platform; it's your global stage. The camera may be small, but your impact can be massive if you know how to own the box."
—Forbes Riley

CHAPTER Z: Zoom

Zoom (noun): *A digital platform that revolutionized communication, making pitching, networking, and closing deals possible from anywhere in the world.*

Zoom. A word that once meant speed and movement has now become synonymous with connection, communication, and opportunity. The 2020 COVID-19 pandemic redefined the way we interact, making it clear that access to people, partnerships, and pitches is now just a click away. Imagine how much more challenging a worldwide lockdown would have been without this technology. We are living in an era where reaching an audience of 10, 100, or even 1,000 people can happen instantly from the comfort of your home. That level of access is unprecedented.

So, how does Zoom impact your pitch? The answer is simple: 55% of communication is non-verbal. The moment you appear on screen, before you even say a word, you are already making an impression. Your background, lighting, eye contact, posture, and even the way you frame yourself on camera, all of these elements send messages to your audience.

Think of a Marvel movie. The actors stand in front of a green screen, pretending to battle intergalactic villains with nothing but their imagination. But once the special effects, sound, and music are added, the audience is transported into an entirely new world. Zoom is your Marvel movie and you are the main character. How you present yourself, your energy, your setup, your confidence, it all creates the experience for your audience.

Television taught me the power of the screen. After years of pitching on live TV, I know that everything in the frame matters.

And now, thanks to Zoom, you have full control over how you appear. Here's how to harness the power of pitching on camera:

1. Open Zoom with your camera on and look at yourself. Do this alone. No judgment. No pressure, just observe.
2. Take a screenshot and analyze your presence.
3. Ask yourself 3 key questions:
   - ❑ Based on how you look, what does this person (you) in the image stand for?
   - ❑ Do I trust this person?
   - ❑ Do I enjoy looking at this person?

Be prepared for discomfort. It's natural. But just like an actor in a superhero suit shooting at an invisible alien, it's not about how you feel; it's about the experience you create for your audience.

When it comes to video communication, presence matters more than you might think. Your energy, posture, and confidence translate through the screen. Have you ever been on a Zoom call where someone looked disengaged, slouched, or had poor lighting? How did that make you feel about their credibility?

Now, compare that to someone who appears well-lit, with a clean background and a confident presence. The difference is night and day.

Whether you're hosting a small business meeting, an online training, or a large-scale summit, making Zoom work for you is essential. Here are my top 5 tips to elevate your virtual presence:

1. Lights, Camera, Action

Think of your Zoom box like your own personal movie screen and every scene needs great lighting. Lighting sets the tone, creates mood, and yes... makes you look like the pro you are.

Avoid overhead lights or desk lamps that cast unflattering shadows. Natural daylight works well, but what happens when you have a meeting at night? Invest in quality lighting whether it's a ring light or a softbox.

Finally what shows up on your screen matters. If your background reveals cluttered bookcases, your messy kitchen, or a pile of laundry, all of that instantly hurts your credibility. With Zoom technology, as if by magic, you can transform your environment to be a high-end penthouse, corner office, or a beachfront living room. Just be sure to make your surroundings match your message.

2. Own the Virtual Connection

Your camera isn't just a lens; it's your communication gateway. Position it at eye level to create a natural, engaging presence. If it's too low, people are staring up at your nose (not a good look). Too high? You'll seem small, like you're sinking into your chair. Aim for a straight-on, professional frame that mirrors an in-person conversation.

The real magic? Eye contact. Instead of looking at yourself on screen (tempting, I know), train yourself to look directly into the camera lens. It might feel unnatural at first, but to your audience, it makes all the difference. When you "lock eyes" with the camera, the listener feels like you're speaking directly to them, not just reading from a screen. This small shift instantly boosts credibility, connection, and engagement.

3. Read the Room to Keep Them Engaged

Engagement isn't automatic on Zoom; you have to create it. The beauty of virtual meetings is that names are right in front of you, making it effortless to personalize interactions. Call people by name, ask direct questions, and encourage real-time participation. A simple, "Who's excited? Drop a 'yes' in the chat!" instantly wakes up the room and pulls people in.

But engagement isn't just about what you say—it's about what you see. Pay attention to body language, even through a screen. Are cameras turning off? Are people glancing at their phones or looking distracted? That's your cue to shake things up. Shift your tone, ask an unexpected question, or inject a bit of humor to recapture their attention. When you read the virtual room and respond in real time, you keep your audience actively involved, making your pitch impossible to ignore.

4. **Your Voice is Your Superpower**

   Your voice isn't just delivering words; it's setting the tone, driving engagement, and influencing perception. A monotone delivery is the fastest way to lose your audience, so bring variation into your speech.

   Energy is contagious. If you sound confident and passionate, they'll lean in, listen, and stay engaged. Eliminate filler words like "um" and "uh"—they dilute your authority. And remember, a smile isn't just something people see; it's something they hear. When you speak with enthusiasm and authenticity, your audience feels it.

5. **Master the Technology**

   Familiarizing yourself with Zoom's features isn't just a nice-to-have... it's essential for a smooth, engaging presentation. Did you know there's a difference between a webinar and a meeting? Webinars allow you to track emails and attendance, making follow-ups effortless. Meetings, on the other hand, let you create breakout rooms where participants can interact in smaller groups, mimicking an in-person experience.

> You want to explore the wide variety of features Zoom has to offer from smoothing out your skin and applying a digital touch of makeup to interacting with a virtual whiteboard and screen-sharing slideshows. The more you master these features, the more confident, polished, and professional you'll appear and the more effective your Zoom call will be.

As someone who's been in business for over 30 years, there has never been a more exciting time to be an entrepreneur. This is the golden age of pitching your ideas to the world. Recently I closed a $100,000 deal in my pajama bottoms and thanks to Zoom, no one knew.

Technology has removed borders and opened doors. Today, I work with students from England to Australia, Mozambique to Malaysia, all from my home studio. Distance is no longer a barrier, and opportunity has never been more accessible.

Zoom isn't just a video platform; it's your stage, your boardroom, and your global connection hub. The way you show up, engage, and leverage its features can make or break your audience's experience. The pandemic lockdown may be over, but Zoom isn't going anywhere. It has evolved beyond business meetings into livestreams, coaching sessions, virtual summits, and worldwide collaborations.

When you master pitching on Zoom, you're not just elevating your presence in virtual meetings—you're building a skill that extends far beyond. Whether it's Facebook Live, Instagram, LinkedIn, YouTube, or any other digital platform, your ability to captivate, connect, and convert will open doors to limitless opportunities.

Let me share a real example. One of my students, a highly accomplished entrepreneur, struggled with pitching to investors over Zoom. In-person, she was magnetic. But online, she lacked confidence, fidgeted, and avoided eye contact. After just one coaching session focusing on Zoom presence, lighting, and storytelling techniques, she closed a six-figure deal on her very next call. The difference? She understood how to *own the screen*.

Your ability to pitch effectively on Zoom isn't just a skill; it's a necessity in today's digital world. Whether you're presenting to investors, hosting webinars, or delivering a keynote, your virtual presence can make or break your success.

Take full advantage of this technology. Refine your on-screen persona. Engage your audience. Perfect your pitch. And most importantly, seize the opportunity to create an unforgettable experience for your viewers.

Because when you master the art of pitching on Zoom, you don't just sell a product or service—you sell *yourself* as a confident, capable, and charismatic leader. And that is the true secret to standing out in the virtual world.

So now the question is, what will you do with what you've learned? Will you just think about it, or will you stand up, speak up, and own your voice? Because the moment you decide to step into your power and master the pitch, everything changes.

Lights. Camera. Pitch. Your future is waiting.

Or
SCAN
HERE

Pitch
Secrets
A to Z

NOW YOU KNOW THE *Secret*

Join The Pitch Secrets "Shhh" Movement!

Win prizes & recognition as a valued member of our mission.

How to Participate

1. Grab your copy of *Pitch Secrets A to Z*
2. Take a "Shhh" photo, finger to your lips
3. Post the photo to your Social Media
4. Hashtag it with #PitchSecrets
5. Share it with friends!

ACKNOWLEDGMENTS

Writing *Pitch Secrets A to Z* has been a labor of love, and this book would not exist without the incredible support, inspiration, and guidance of so many wonderful people.

For years, like many of you, I operated as a lone wolf, a solopreneur, believing that if I just worked harder, pushed longer, and did it all myself, success would follow. But I've come to realize the undeniable truth in the saying: *If you want to go fast, go alone. If you want to go far, go together.*

A great Dream Team is the secret ingredient to lasting success. With the right people by your side, those who challenge you, support you, and share the vision—you can accomplish more than you ever imagined. I am deeply grateful for those who have walked this path with me, contributing their talents, insights, and dedication to making this book, this movement, and this mission a reality.

First and foremost, Makenna, your belief in me and our mother-daughter empire fuels my passion every day. You are my greatest supporter, my fiercest champion, and the reason this book, our training, and our thriving business exist.

With the kind of vision and determination beyond her years, she led the charge, helping me take everything I had spent a lifetime mastering and transformed it into a global coaching movement. She saw the opportunity before I did, pushed forward when I hesitated, and refused to let me play small.

Makenna, this book is as much yours as it is mine. Your heart for impact has shaped every word, every lesson, every success story that has come from this journey. I couldn't have done this without you, and I wouldn't want to.

To my son, Ryker, you are the light of my life and the perfect yin to my yang. Your academic prowess, wisdom, and wit challenge and inspire me daily. With a heart as big as your intellect, you navigate life with a quiet strength that leaves a lasting impact on everyone you meet, making the world and my life so much richer.

I want to give a special shoutout to my mom and dad, who left this physical world in 2001 but continue to live on in my heart. Your unconditional love always pushed me to exceed boundaries, seize opportunities, and create possibilities where there were none. Through my writing and my speeches, your legacy lives on, motivating millions.

To my life partner, Joshua Self, your strength goes beyond muscle; it's in your heart, your unwavering support, and the way you lift me higher every day. As a world-class fitness champion, a 3D graphic artist, and my rock, you inspire me in ways I never imagined. But above all, you surround me with love and laughter. Joshua, I love you now and forever. Thank you!

To my incredible team at The Forbes Factor and to everyone who has been part of this book's journey, from concept to completion, thank you for believing in the power of the pitch and for helping me bring this vision to life.

I have a special shoutout to the very talented and compassionate Nicole Zemaitis, whose willingness to burn the midnight oil is nothing short of heroic. You've left your fingerprints on a legacy that will impact lives. Now and forever. Thank you!

I want to thank everyone in the Forbes Factor Family—from my Inner Circle members to Pitch Like a Pro students and Next Level Speaker graduates. Our community has grown to over 100,000 strong, filled with entrepreneurs who've trusted me to teach you how to use your voice and share your message with the world. Watching you step up, pitch with confidence, and succeed in your missions has been one of the greatest honors of my career. Seeing your progress—one by one—has brought me more joy than I can put into words. Thank you for being part of this journey. Let's keep Forbes'ing it, together.

To Sandy and Marilyn, your final review of this book was not only meticulous; it was a gift. You've been more than students; you've been loyal supporters, compassionate friends, and shining examples of what it means to show up fully.

To Ann Landstrom, award-winning photographer, thank you for capturing the image on the cover of this book and, more importantly, the essence of who I am. Your artistry made this more than a photo. I am proud to have your brilliance as part of this legacy.

To the brands, companies, and visionaries who entrusted me with their message, products, and dreams, thank you. From global powerhouses to passionate entrepreneurs, who handed me their product with the hope that I could help bring it to life, through a magical pitch, just know that your trust has been my greatest honor and our successes, the highlight of my career.

To the legends of infomercials, it's been a privilege to work with you! If I didn't mention you by name, you know who you are. Thank you for cementing forever the power of the pitch on TV.

To my dear friend and mentor, Les Brown, your wisdom and example taught me that speaking from the heart is the ultimate pitch.

To the people who believed in me throughout my life, a heartfelt thank you for supporting me and sharing this journey with me. There's too many to mention by name; you know who you are, and thank you.

And finally, to you, the bold inventors, relentless entrepreneurs, and visionaries who pick up this book—thank you for daring to dream. You are the heartbeat of innovation and the champions of change. My hope is that *Pitch Secrets A to Z* becomes more than just a book on your shelf, but a powerful tool in your journey to transform your ideas into reality, your message into a movement, and your pitch into a legacy.

Your voice deserves to be heard.

With immense gratitude,

Forbes Riley

DR. FORBES RILEY

The "Queen of Pitch" 2x TEDx Speaker

Not only did Forbes write the book on Pitching, she delivered the TEDx Talk.

Watch the TEDx Talk
Scan the QR Code

ABOUT THE AUTHOR

Dr. Forbes Riley is a trailblazing entrepreneur, award-winning TV host, and the undisputed Queen of Pitch, with over $2.5 billion in product sales. A pioneer of the infomercial industry, she's hosted 197 national shows; appeared on QVC, HSN, and major networks; and coached over 100,000 students in the art of high-impact communication and sales. Forbes is a 2-time TEDx speaker, bestselling author, and a Hall of Fame–inducted fitness icon, known for her signature product SpinGym and her magnetic stage presence. From pitching with legends like Jack LaLanne and Billy Mays to mentoring the next generation of entrepreneurs, Forbes continues to redefine what's possible—on screen, on stage, and in life.

I'm beyond grateful you joined me on this journey.

Whether you're just starting out or already making waves, your willingness to grow, learn, and pitch with purpose is what sets you apart. I wrote this book for you, to help you find your voice, own your value, and share your message with the world.

I've put together powerful bonus resources to support your next steps, including video trainings, templates, and exclusive tools.

If this book helped you shift your mindset, clarify your pitch, or take bold new action—I'd love to hear from you.

Your feedback means everything. We would love for you to share a review and a picture of you holding the book.
Simply email us at Support@TeamForbesRiley.com.

With love and belief in your brilliance,

Forbes Riley

You have a message. The world is waiting.